Civil War And Living History Reenacting

IN CHARACTER
Ernestine Johnson, as Harriet Tubman, at the 2003 Reenactment of the
Florida Civil War Battle of Olustee, fought February 20, 1864.

CIVIL WAR AND LIVING HISTORY REENACTING

ABOUT "PEOPLE OF COLOR"

How To Begin - What To Wear - Why Reenact

Illustrated by
Gina Gillislee Hickman
and
Joel Van Fears, Sr.

Mary L. Jackson Fears

HERITAGE BOOKS
2012

HERITAGE BOOKS
AN IMPRINT OF HERITAGE BOOKS, INC.

Books, CDs, and more—Worldwide

For our listing of thousands of titles see our website
at
www.HeritageBooks.com

Published 2012 by
HERITAGE BOOKS, INC.
Publishing Division
100 Railroad Ave. #104
Westminster, Maryland 21157

Copyright © 2004 Mary L. Jackson Fears

Direct correspondence to:
Mary L. Jackson Fears
722 Mercedes Avenue
Daytona Beach, FL 32114
e-mail: jmar30@aol.com
website: http://members.aol.com/jmar30/SlaveResearch/

Other Heritage Books by the author:
Slave Ancestral Research: It's Something Else

Cover design by Joel V. Fears, Sr.

All rights reserved. No part of this book may be reproduced or transmitted in any form or by any means, electronic or mechanical, including photocopying, recording or by any information storage and retrieval system without written permission from the author, except for the inclusion of brief quotations in a review.

International Standard Book Numbers
Paperbound: 978-0-7884-2513-4
Clothbound: 978-0-7884-9196-2

DEDICATION

To my most loving and supportive husband, Joel V. Fears, Sr.,
my two sons: John H. Anderson, Jr., Joel V. Fears, Jr., my grandson,
John H. Anderson, III, and the remaining descendants of
The Jackson-Moore and Ewing-Denman Families. Also in
loving memory of my daughter, Julie LaVera Anderson.

It is my hope that this publication will serve to: stimulate more appreciation for the sacrificial struggles of our ancestors to gain the *freedoms* that all in present generations enjoy; and most importantly, to increase the desire of all people to learn more about the history of African-Americans in the development of this country.

CONTENTS

List of Illustrations viii
Foreword x
Acknowledgments xi
Introduction xiii

Why Civilian Civil War Reenacting

Prologue 1

1. Civilian Civil War Reenacting *For and About* "People of Color" 5

Who They Were: the "People of Color" During the Civil War

Who They Were: the "People of Color" During the Civil War 9
"Free People of Color" or *fpc* 11
Slaves: Field Hands and House Servants 14

2. Life on Southern Plantations During the Civil War 21

What They Did: the "People of Color" During the Civil War

3. Civilian "People of Color" Who Served in Non-combat Roles 33
Harriet Tubman, Scout, Nurse, and Guide 37
Elizabeth Bowser, Spy 41
Charlotte Forten, Teacher 43
Mary Kelsey Peake, Teacher 46
Elizabeth Keckley, Modiste to Mary Todd Lincoln 47
Susie King Taylor, Nurse 51
Sojourner Truth, Abolitionist, Supporter 55
Frederick Douglass, Recruiter 57
Military Service: Henry McNeal Turner, Chaplain 59 Robert Smalls, Seaman 61

What They Wore: the "People of Color" During the Civil War

4. The Slave Seamstress 67
Clothing of "Free People of Color" 71
Plates: Fabric Patterns; Boys' and Girls' 1860s Style Clothing, *Follow page 80*

5. What to Wear, Making Do with What You Have 85
Where to Look for What to Wear 89

Why Reenact About "People of Color" at Civil War Reenactments

6. Why Become a Civil War Reenactor 93
"Who me? I don't want to do that." 95
"Why I Remain a Reenactor after My First Experience" 97
"I'll Never Forget My First Olustee Reenactment Experience" 101

What's It About, "Military Reenacting," at Civil War Reenactments

7. Reenacting in Military Units 107
Meet Civil War Reenactors: Mel Reid, 115; Clifford Pierce and John Peden 119
So You Want to Get Involved in Civil War Military Reenacting,
but Don't Know Where or How to Begin 121

What Is Remembered

8. Reminiscences from a Civil War Reenactment 127
Epilogue 131
Bibliography 132
Appendix 141
Index 151

ILLUSTRATIONS

Figures   Page

Frontispiece, Ernestine Johnson as Harriet Tubman

1. WHY CIVILIAN CIVIL WAR REENACTING Civil War Cannon
2. Contrabands at Cook Tent   *Faces page* 1
3. 1860s Dress Style   4
4. Alma McMillan in 1860s Dress with Swiss Belt   4
5. Oscar Patterson, Jacqueline Pierce (In Flowered Dress)   4
6. Clifford Pierce and Jacqueline Pierce (In Dress with Swiss Belt)   4

7. WHO THEY WERE: "THE PEOPLE OF COLOR"....Anisha Cotton
                                                        Follows page 8

8-11. WHO THEY WERE: SLAVES, HOUSE SLAVES, "FREE PEOPLE OF COLOR,"
      MILITARY "PEOPLE OF COLOR"   *Faces page* 9
12. Mrs. James Babcock, a Business Woman Baker   10
13. The Desolate Home   18
14. SLAVE REMOVAL
    LEAVING CHARLESTON ON THE CITY BEING BOMBARDED.   20

15. WHAT THEY DID: THE "PEOPLE OF COLOR"....Susie King Taylor   31
16. Reenactors as Skilled Craftsmen:
    Joel V. Fears Sr., a Cooper; Joel V. Fears, Jr., a Carpenter   32
17. Sarah Rone as a "Free Person of Color"   36
18. Ernestine Johnson as Harriet Tubman   37
19. Harriet Tubman   39
20. Teen-age Sisters Mary and Emily Edmondson   40
21. Virginia Smith as Mary Elizabeth Bowser   41
22. Merceda Nicholson as Charlotte Forten   43
23. Teen and Pre-Teen 1860s Style Dresses   45
24. Loretta Dabbs as Mary Kelsey Peake, Teacher   46
25. Yvette Birdsong as Elizabeth Keckley   47
26. Azza Thames as Susie King Taylor   51
27. Unidentified Woman   54
28. Sojourner Truth with Abraham Lincoln   55
29. Matherlyn Smith as Sojourner Truth   56
30. Frederick Douglass   57
31. Rev. Michael A. Frazier as Chaplain Henry McNeal Turner   59
32. A "Free Family of Color"   60
33. Kenneth O. Mitchell as Robert Smalls   61
34. Robert Smalls, Captain of the Union Gunboat, "Planter"   62
35. Slave Woman in Apron   64

36. WHAT THEY WORE: "PEOPLE OF COLOR"....Jane Patterson   65
37. Contrabands at Follie's Farm, 1863   66
38. Crocheted Cape   69
39. Joyce E. Booker as a Slave Seamstress   69
40. House Slave Servants Received Hand-Me-Down Clothing   70
    Sharon R. Yates and Mary J. Fears

ILLUSTRATIONS

Figures	Page
41. Teenage Nurse, Aunt Lizzie	72
42. Child's Dress with Cape	73
43. Wool Cape	73
44. Dress Accessories: Bonnet, Purses, Gloves, Bodice, Under Sleeves, Crocheted Collars, Neck Tie	74
45. 1860s Hats and Hairstyles	76
46. Suit Style of the 1860s	78
47. Rev. John Jasper	78
48. Janome Ward	79
49. Woman with Boy	79
50. Jane Patterson	80

PLATES
FABRIC PATTERNS — *Follows page 80*
51. BOYS' 1860s STYLE CLOTHING — *Follows FABRIC PATTERNS*
52. GIRLS' 1860s STYLE CLOTHING — *Follows Boy's Clothing page*

53. Young Reenactors | 81
54. Making Do With What You Have For An Adult Male | 84
55. Making Do With What You Have, The Dress After the Change | 87
56. 1860s Dresses for Teens | 88
57. Union and Confederate Reenactors at The 2003 Battle of Olustee Reenactment | 90

58. WHY REENACT ABOUT "PEOPLE OF COLOR"....Yvette Birdsong | 91
59. Jackson, the Drummer Boy and Reenactor Jesus Laino as Jackson | 92
60. Gordon, an Infantry Soldier | 94
61. Reenactors Ernestine Johnson and Douglas Jarrett | 101

62. WHAT'S IT ABOUT, "MILITARY REENACTING"....
    An Unidentified Black Soldier and Wife | 105
63. Nicholas Biddle | 106
64. Reenactor Mel Turner, 54th Massachusetts Volunteer Infantry | 111
65. Reenactors: Karl King, Leon Vaughn and John Peden | 112
66. Union Reenactors At Rest | 112
67. Reenactor Pvt. Mel Reid, 54th Massachusetts Volunteer Infantry, Co. B | 114
68. Reenactor John Peden, 54th Massachusetts Volunteer Infantry, Co. F | 118
69. Reenactor Chaplain Clifford Pierce, 54th Mass. Volunteer Infantry, Co. F | 118

Female Contrabands in Union Service
70. Barbara Brockington with Union Reenactors | 120
71. Pinkie A. Caldwell | 120

72. WHAT IS REMEMBERED, Loretta Dabbs | 125
73. Reenactor Mary Fears | 126
74. Reenactor Pepper R. Booker, Visiting a Sutler at Bishop's Farm Reenactment | 154

FOREWORD

This book is designed to teach others how to gain a better perspective of the image of becoming a reenactor. It also improves the ability to express one's identity. Learning is an element that is common to all reenactors.

Understanding the basics is explored within the book. Learning to develop the messages is based on the point of view one wishes to personify. Learning the ways to define and adjust the tone of a reenactor is an offer, tip and technique to the African-American. Those have been placed within the manuscript.

In general, studies have demonstrated that reenactors are self-identifying, are happier; less stressful and have a greater longevity of fun. But before one becomes a reenactor and gets into his persona of living history, he must learn how, what and why. These are covered within the text.

Process is a term reenactors use to refer to the way one evolves. *How*, is often taken as the form of a description of *what* is the self-identity of his or her impression. *What*, is the harder question to answer and *what* someone should do, if he or she is convinced that reenacting is for him or herself. The problem comes from each situation and it has so many variables, like what he or she is going to wear. That situation of what to wear can become a long or short-term solution. *Why* reenact is a key consideration to the solution. There needs to be that African-American person in history. He or she enrolls the behavior of that person. Then the need and the behavior are equal in the solution.

The bottom line of reenacting is the style. One needs to make his own evaluation. The situation of helping with the style and evaluation is the guidance within this book.

ERIC J. HAGUE
Sutlery Coordinator
Battle of Olustee Reenactments

ACKNOWLEDGMENTS

The one person most deserving of my sincerest thanks is my husband, Joel V. Fears, Sr. Not one of my writing projects could have ever been successfully completed without his love and encouragement together with his most needed travel assistance and technical support with the computer. Thanks to my "WBW" colleagues and Florida AAHGS members for support. Extra special thanks is expressed to Joe Vetter for reading the manuscript and the selection of teenage model Anisha Cotton. I sincerely thank Anisha and each of the models who posed for photographs. I feel deeply gracious and thankful for the friendship and support of Wesley McMillan and his wife Alma, who evolved as my consultant in the use of 1860 fashions from her unique clothing collection. Thanks to Rick Lovinsky, Joyce Booker and Toni Cancel for making clothing items. Thanks to Emily Croom for finding the impossible.

I am grateful to: Sallie Shelton Culver and Jane Harmon for editing the manuscript; to Jason Caros, Emma Grace Burke, and Harriet Fulmore for reading the manuscript and giving editorial comments.

Special thanks is expressed for the welcoming spirit and support of Eric Hague and Martha Nelson of the staff of the Olustee Battle Reenactment. To the following sutlers, a special thanks is expressed for the use of their Civil War wares and implements used in the photographs taken at Olustee and at the Reenactment of the Battle for Lake Helen at Bishop's Farm: Mike Luck of Colonial Smith & Forge; Joanne B. Kurtright, Period Seamstress; Bob and Addie Smethurst of Packrat Bob's Sutlery; Terry Cummings of Peninsula Sutlery; Kathryn L. Simmons, The Senators Lady; Wilahmena Lauramore of Southern Family Impressions; Celestine Graham of Stitches Wood & More; and Sutlersuch. I am especially thankful to the Confederate and Union soldier reenactors photographed at the Reenactments at Olustee, FL and at Bishop's Farm in Lake Helen, FL.

Photograph credits:
  Cover: Joel V. Fears, Sr.; Chris Livingston: Frontispiece

Ada Tharp Album, PH038 CL Sonnichsen, Spec. Collections Dept., Univ. of Texas: 105

Joel V. Fears, Photographer: 4, 32, 36, 37, 41, 43, 46, 47, 51, 56, 59, 61, 69, 70, 73, 74, 76, 81, 84, 87, 90, 91, 92, 101, 111, 112, 120, 125, 154

Gina Hickman: 45, 88 and other pen and ink drawings in the text

Joy Wallace Dickinson: 101; Melicent Remy: 79; Oberlin College: 65, 80

Sixth Mt. Zion Baptist Church: 78

U.S. Military History Institute (USMHI): 66, 106

Library of Congress (LC): *Faces* p.1, 18, 31, 39, 40, 55, 57, 62, 79, 92, 94

Valentine Museum: 72; New Hampshire Historical Society: 64

Deborah Cooney Collection: 60, 78; Essex Peabody Museum Institute: 10

INTRODUCTION

I decided to write a book titled <u>Civil War and Living History Reenacting About "People of Color" How to Begin – What to Wear – Why Reenact.</u> Why did I make that decision? The prime motivation was my first reenactment experience at the 2002 Florida Civil War Battle of Olustee Reenactment.

My discovery of reenacting as an effective way of telling an important part of the history of African-Americans "the way it was" provided the impetus. Through reenacting, all who gave service in the War Between the States, whether in the military or as civilians in non-combat roles *come alive*. Reenactments are "living history" events. The Union won the war, but all the people who gave service in it may not be represented at Civil War reenactments. Not only did black men wear the military uniforms of the Union and fight valiantly, but also serving were black civilians. Throughout the text, "people of color" refers to black people, both military and civilians. Who were the black civilians who lived during the Civil War years, 1861-1865, and what did they do? The civilian population included, African slaves and their descendants, and others identified in 1860s' records as "free people of color." Within documents of the period, it can be discovered who they were and what they did. My research identified names of a few civilian "people of color" who gave service in the Civil War. They are suggested as characters for reenactment roles. Continued research will reveal the identity of other black civilians who served in the Civil War.

One purpose of this guide is to inspire African-Americans to attend Civil War battle reenactments and become reenactors by representing either military roles or civilians in non-combat roles. Reenacting is fun, a hobby that enables persons to become "living historians." When one is costumed in the clothing styles of ancestors, it provides a personally rewarding vicarious experience and the *good feeling* of knowing that more of African-American history is being told. A second important purpose of this book is to provide an extensive annotated bibliography of reference sources both for Civil War reenactors and for school library book collections.

One author's examination of school social studies textbooks revealed that many details were omitted from African-American participation in the Civil War. James W. Loewen, in <u>Lies My Teacher Taught Me, Everything Your American History Textbook Got Wrong</u>, (NY: Simon & Schuster, 1995) directed readers' attention to distortions, omissions, and often, simple untruths printed in American history textbooks used in today's schools. His book should be read, as suggested by Howard Zinn, by "every teacher, every student of history and every citizen." (Quoted from the cover.)

The books included in the bibliographies that follow each chapter are listed as authentic sources for further reading. These titles will suggest topics pertinent to students for their "living history" projects. Biographical stories of "people of color" who gave service in the Civil War provide information with human interest appeal and will extend readers' understanding of the war. Many titles in the chapter bibliographies cover the history of African-Americans beginning with the African slave trade followed by numerous historic events extending to the present. My text, however, focuses primarily upon the services rendered by "people of color" *during* the Civil War and was written with a description of what their everyday lives were like and how they were affected by the war.

The books listed in the bibliographies provide background information that reenactors need to know in order to explain the character roles they will portray. This information includes the life experiences of slaves and of free people, their occupational skills, clothing styles, and living conditions. The book titles which are starred (*) are the most helpful, especially those which feature photographs of 1860s style clothing needed for reenacting character roles in Civil War and other "living history" events. Reenactors are *required* to wear the appropriate clothing styles of the Civil War era.

This book is a reference source in education with special interest for school library media specialists, teachers and their students in American history classes, as well as persons who are reenactors. It is a practical guide. Special emphasis is placed on the valuable contributions made by African-Americans, (continuously referred to in the text as "people of color") during the Civil War. Rather than dwell upon the many evils of the slavery system, the focus of this book is upon how reenacting presents a way to *celebrate* the heroic deeds of black people. However, to relate pertinent facts about the impact of the Civil War, it must be reported that some cruel punishments were meted out to family members when slave men escaped to serve the Union.

In summary, the dual purpose of this guide is to provide incentives for people of color to become reenactors and most importantly, to provide a list of resources that present the history of African-Americans. To fulfill the requirements of those two purposes, a description of plantation life is presented with quotes from slave narratives and Civil War documents. Occupations of slaves and "free people of color" are presented. The primary aim is to present to readers all that is needed to begin the hobby of reenacting and to provide illustrations of appropriate wearing apparel. The guide cannot be considered a treatise on the evils of slavery, nor the rights and wrongs of the

Civil War. It does not attempt to present a discussion on the causes of the war, nor the controversial issues related to the conflict. Rather, the primary focus is to provide the reader with an understanding of what life was like on the plantations and small farms for slaves during the Civil War and what life was like for "free people of color."

As I researched for this book, I was strongly affected by the Civil War experiences of black people. I felt tenaciously caught up in my ancestral past. Noah A. Trudeau's <u>Like Men of War</u>; (NY: Little, Brown & Co., 1998) and Benjamin Quarles' <u>The Negro in the Civil War</u> (Boston: Little Brown & Co., 1969) had great influence. These books intensified my desire to know more about the role of black people in the Civil War. In books like those, written candidly about the Civil War, readers are exposed to the factual history of African-Americans.

Readers will notice that a specific section is not designated in the back matter for Notes. Instead, I chose to place footnotes at the end of chapters and placed the page numbers of quotes within the text. I made this decision to "Avoid exasperating readers with endnotes consisting of nothing but a page number or just 'Ibid.' When a number of references are made to a single work, page or line numbers may be given in the text, enclosed in parenthesis. The note accompanying the first appearance of the work should give the full citation." (From <u>The Chicago Manual of Style, 13th Edition.</u> Chicago: University of Chicago Press, 1982. p.412.)

Special notes for reenactors precede the footnotes in several chapters. A brief bibliography, which covers the chapter topics, is printed at the end of several chapters for the convenience of readers. An additional, more comprehensive bibliography, is printed at the end of the text.

Since this is a guide for assisting reenactors in the selection of 1860s style clothing, photographs of presently active reenactors wearing their reenactment outfits are featured within the text. The pen and ink drawings of 1860s style clothing are based upon photographs in books listed in the bibliographies that feature clothing styles of the Civil War era.

Why Civilian Civil War Reenacting

Civil War Cannon
Tredegar Iron Works, Richmond, VA

Fig. 2. Contrabands at a Union Cook Tent in Culpepper, VA during November, 1863
Library of Congress # B8171-221

PROLOGUE

The following scene is in the remote area of a southern plantation. A slave mother bends over her sewing. It is about ten o'clock at night. After a day of field work, she sits upon a slave carpenter's crudely constructed chair making a quilt to warm the three remaining of her six children. She sews by the light of a pine wood torch and the smoldering embers in the fireplace. Her dozing eight year old son holds the torch.

Within the drab confines of a wooden floorless cabin, her mind carries thoughts of her husband who fathered her six children. He had run away from an adjoining plantation two nights before to join the Yankees. She wonders if he reached the troops or if he were followed by the pattyrollers (patrollers), caught, and punished or even shot for having fled to the Yankees. She has no way of knowing; only time would tell. (*Pattyrollers* was the name used by the slaves.)

With a sigh, she touches her tear-stained face, remembering the night he left: the final good-byes, the tight embrace, the last glance at his children lying asleep on a pallet on the dirt floor. He dared not awaken them. Perhaps hope will bring them together again.

When her eyes can no longer remain open, she breathes an exhausted sigh of fatigue as her body falls unto a cotton mattress ticking stuffed with corn shucks. To reach her resting place, one bare foot stumbles over the children sleeping soundly beneath her.

Her bed hangs by ropes attached to a smoke-blackened wall where clay oozes from within its cracks to keep out the moist cold of a winter's night. Too tired to kneel, she whispers in bed a mournful prayer for her husband and the oft-repeated murmuring of hope that freedom will come soon. Maybe, just maybe, all that's going on will bring it to pass.

Her limbs succumb to sleep for hours too short to count. At 5:00 A.M., from the outside darkness comes the sharp blast of the slave driver's horn. It snatches her body and drags it awake. With the dawn, another grueling day begins. The old woman nurse, Aunt Sally, will take care of her youngest children. She will see them late in the evening. Her oldest, the eight year old, rubbing his eyes awake, whines for the want of sleep. He will go with her to the field to pull weeds and fetch pails of water.

In the cabin scene of the slave mother bending over a quilt, and in the narrative which follows of a North Carolina former slave, is the revelation of what happened during the Civil War. Thousands of slaves left the plantations and fled to freedom within the ranks of Union soldiers.

Prologue

Once within their ranks, they labored long and hard giving support services to the Union in return for that freedom. Therein lies the justification for civilian reenactors. Slave people took the war as their path to freedom.

What about the fortunate few *fpc or* "free people of color?" Free blacks, about 182,000 of them, were also affected by the ravages of the war. Although free, they had always been the target of harassment and had suffered as victims under restrictive laws that placed them only a slight notch above those in bondage with meagerly better living conditions. As free blacks in the North, they were free to exercise their choice in matters about the war. However, in the South, the situation was not the same.

Reenactors who vicariously experience the plight and subsequent actions of both groups, those in bondage and the "free" during the Civil War, will become aware of their importance in reenactment roles.

Excerpts from the Slave Narrative of John C. Bectom (about 75 years old)

"My name is John C. Bectom. I was born October 7, 1862,[1] near Fayetteville, Cumberland County, North Carolina....My father first belonged to Robert Wooten of Craven County, NC. Then he was sold by the Wootens to the Bectoms of Wayne County, near Goldsboro, the county seat. My mother first belonged to the McNeills of Cumberland County. Miss Mary McNeill married a McFadden, and her parents gave my mother to Mis' Mary. Mis' Mary's daughter in time married Ezekiel King. My grandmother was named Lucy Murphy. She belonged to the Murphys. All the slaves were given off to the children of the family as they married....

"They fed us mighty good. The food was well cooked. They gave the slaves an acre of ground to plant and they could sell the crop and have the money. The work on this acre was done on moonshiny nights and holidays. Sometimes slaves would steal the marster's chickens or a hog and slip off to another plantation and have it cooked. We had plenty of clothes and one pair o'shoes a year. You had to take care of them because you only got one pair a year. They were given at Christmas every year. The clothes were made on the plantation....

"I remember seeing the Yankees near Fayetteville. They shot a bomb shell at Wheeler's Cavalry and it hit near me and buried in the ground. Wheeler's Cavalry came first and ransacked the place. They got all the valuables they could, and burned the bridge, the covered bridge over Cape Fear River, but when the Yankees got there, they had pontoon bridge to cross on--all those provision wagons and such. When they passed our place, it was in the morning. They nearly scared me to death. They passed right by our door, Sherman's Army. They began passing, so the folks said, at 9 o'clock in the mornin'. At 9 o'clock at night, they were passin' our door on foot. They said there were two hundred and fifty thousan' o' them passed. Some camped in my Marster's old fiel'. A Yankee caught one of my marster's shoats and cut off one of the hind quarters, gave it to me and told me to carry and give it to my mother. I was so small I could not tote it, so I drug it to her. I called her when I got in hollering distance of the house and she came and got it....At that time Jeff Davis money was plentiful. My mother had about $1000. It was so plentiful it was called Jeff Davis shucks.

"My mother bought a pair of shoes, and put them in a chest. A Yankee came and took the shoes and wore them off, leaving his in their place.

"They tol' us we were free. Sometimes the Marster would get cruel to the slaves if they acted like they were free. Mat Holmes, a slave, was wearing a ball and chain as a punishment for running away. Marster Ezekial King put it on him. He has slept in the bed with me, wearing that ball and chain. The cuff had imbedded in his leg--it was swollen so. This was right after the Yankees came through. Mat Holmes had run away with the ball and chain on him and was in the woods then. He hid out, staying with us at night until August. Then my mother took him to the Yankee garrison at Fayetteville. A Yankee officer then took him to a blacksmith shop and had the ball and chain cut off his leg.

"The Marsters would tell the slaves to go to work, that they were not free, that they still belonged to them, but one would drop out and leave, then another. There was little work done on the farm, and finally most of the slaves learned they were free.

"Abraham Lincoln was one of the greatest men that ever lived.[2] (See Appendix B, Lincoln's Letter to Joshua F. Speed, August 24, 1855.) He was the cause of us slaves being free. No doubt about that. I didn't think anything of Jeff Davis. He tried to keep us in slavery. I think slavery was an injustice--not right.

"Our privilege is to live right, and live according to the teachings of the Bible, to treat our fellowman right. To do this, I feel we should belong to some religious organization and live as near right as we know how."

---

1. From North Carolina Slave Narratives recorded in the WPA Writers Project in the 1930s. *The birth year, as remembered by a 75-year old former slave, cannot be taken as factual.

2. See Appendix B for quotes from the chapter titled, "Lincoln and the Negroes," in <u>Lincoln, His Words and His World</u>, compiled by the Editors of *County Beautiful,* Waukesha, Wisconsin, MCMLXV.

STYLES WORN BY "FREE PEOPLE OF COLOR"

Fig. 3. 1860s Style Dark Print Dress With Hat.

Fig. 4. Dress With Wide Swiss Belt. Points made to go upwards between the breasts and downward at waist front.

Fig. 5. 1860s Style Flowered Print Dress

Fig.6. Solid color dress with Swiss belt worn with cotton long sleeved blouse, cape and hat.

Chapter 1
Civilian Civil War Reenacting *For and About* "People of Color"

In its issues, *The Civil War Courier,* a monthly newspaper, announces in bold print the calendar dates and places of Civil War battle reenactments, thereby extending open invitations to reenactors and visitors alike. Attendance at a reenactment sends first-time visitors home in a state of awe exclaiming loudly, "Is that the way they fought? My gracious!"

No doubt, they have been impressed with the vast numbers of men reenactors dressed in Confederate gray and Union blue engaged in battle. A visitor who questions a reenactor, "Where are you from?" might hear answers that indicate that the reenactors could be from any state in the Union. Another visitor might ask, "Where did you get this thing and where do you keep it?" as he stands close to one of the large cannons, which roll on wheels and which produce loud blasts as they are fired during pre-battle demonstrations. Answers to such questions are amazing. One response was, "I built it and I keep it in my garage!"

Glancing at the passing scenes of civilian reenactors, first-time visitors and old timers see men, women, and children dressed in Civil War period clothing strolling along smiling graciously. Although unspoken, an invitation beckons, "Come and join us. You can be a reenactor too." Why would anyone respond to an invitation to become a reenactor? The response stated simply is: to help bring history alive for the education of people.

The states' Civil War population included "free people of color" or fpc and those in bondage. *(fpc, is the Federal Census identification.)* Representatives from these two groups should be among the strolling citizens to complete scenes at all reenactments. If they are not, or if there are only a few in number, easy steps taken can assure that many people of color will be participants at future reenactments. All that one needs to do to become a reenactor is to locate and contact the program planners. Next steps include informing the planners of one's personal interest and then reading about reenacting, 1860s style clothing and people of color in the Civil War. Then select a character to read about and observe how the selected character dressed. <u>Civil War And Living History Reenacting, About "People of Color," How To Begin, What To Wear, Why Reenact</u> is a practical guide for beginners.

Reenactors interpret the roles of individuals who were involved in historic events. Authentic clothing and accessories of the period are most essential for reenactors. An effort should be made to view photographs of people who lived during the period of the reenactment or "living history" experience.

Arranging period hair styles, along with wearing period clothing, will help reenactors or living historians slip into the past and really feel the roles portrayed. Reenactors may expect questions about their clothing and should be prepared to answer them. Clothing styles reflected the social status and life styles of the people in every period in history.

During the Civil War era, there was a distinct difference in the styles of clothing worn by people in bondage, "free people of color" and by people in the planter or ruling class in southern states and wealthy people in northern states. A reenactor would be expected to explain who made his/her clothing and how fabric was acquired and distributed. Spinning, weaving, fabric dyeing, and handicrafts like sewing, knitting and crocheting occupied much of women's time. Such skills would need to be explained along with a description of the various items worn by women like hoops, hats, purses, shoes, etc. Children's and men's clothing styles, as well as occupations of men and women, should be described in brief talks.

Just as wearing period clothing of the historic time of a reenactment aids civilian reenactors, the men who serve as military reenactors in Civil War reenactments, are expected to wear uniforms and live like soldiers. They are expected to use only items from the Civil War era, so that they can, as nearly as possible, experience what it was like to serve in the Civil War. Thus, they gain a better understanding of what it may have felt like to have been a soldier in the Civil War.

Reenactors are expected to give brief talks and answer questions graciously. Rather than giving wrong information, a simple "I don't know" is an acceptable response with an added, "But I shall try to find the answer for the next time someone asks that question." At reenactments, small groups of people will gather at different times. It is a good idea to be prepared with much information. Reenactors should be prepared to vary their talks with more than one piece of information.

A reenactor or living historian should always avoid arguing with a viewer. The simple explanation of a fact should be stated and the source document cited in a courteous tone of voice. Then the verbal exchange should end.

Portrayed historic figures do not have to be famous as there were common, ordinary people living at the time of the Civil War and at other great historic events. They helped to make history and also deserve recognition. "...during the (Civil) War, there were more than 200,000 Negro civilians in the service of the Northern Armies as laborers, cooks, teamsters, and servants."(1,p.94) To include them in "living history" settings will give viewers an even broader and different perspective of a specific time and historic event.

Reenactors in living history settings make the past seem alive and interesting. Reenacting offers an excellent opportunity for teaching and learning. It is a personally rewarding hobby that offers fun and enjoyment for viewers and reenactors alike.

What Is It Really About, Civilian Reenacting?

Reenacting as a civilian in a historic event like the Civil War, while assuming the role of a significant character, is an excellent tool for teaching history. It is a way of reliving the past for the reenactor and developing a clearer understanding and knowledge of a bygone era for all who witness the event. To be effective as a reenactor, one must have a general knowledge of the time in which the historic event occurred and dress appropriately for the character he/she portrays. In addition to those requirements, also helpful, is reading books written about living history and interpretation to assure essential preparation for success as reenactors or living historians.

The one best way to equip oneself for the reenacting role is to do research. Extensive reading of documents about the historic events assures the possibility of being authentic. The reenactor needs to be prepared, as persons in attendance at reenactments may ask questions or even question parts of the presentation. The reenactor, to be effective, must feel confident in his or her portrayal of his subject. Reenacting is really role-playing. It brings living history to light and must accurately reflect historical facts.

Some reenactors may decide to "become" the historic figure by not only dressing as the character would have dressed, but also by adapting his or her speech patterns and speaking in the manner common to that character's time period. This means that the reenactor speaks in the first person at all times, even in conversations with others. His or her answers to questions must not reflect modern thinking. Answers to questions must be given in a manner that reflects the way life was during the portrayed character's life time.

The most common approach to the reenactor's character is to use the third person in speech. That means to speak *about* the character. Wearing the appropriate style of clothing worn by the character portrayed will establish the character in the minds of viewers at events. For beginning reenactors, this latter approach is the easiest.

---

1. Quarles, Benjamin. The Negro In The Civil War. Boston: Little, Brown & Co., 1969.

Bibliography

The following are suggested titles for reading about living history interpretation and Civil War reenacting.

Anderson, Jay. <u>The Living History Source book.</u> Nashville: American Association for State and Local History Press, 1985.
    This title is highly suggested reading for its comprehensive coverage of living history and interpretation.

Daily, Bryan. <u>The Basics: How To Get Started in Civil War Reenacting.</u> Austin, IN. Self-published.
    Available through interlibrary loans.

Hadden, R. Lee. <u>Reliving the Civil War, A Reenactor's Handbook.</u> Mechanicsburg, PA: Stackpole Books, 1996.
    A detailed bibliography is given for the book's chapters which include: "Civilian Reenacting," "Reenactment for Infantry" and "Union and Confederate Soldier Life." It is highly recommended for military Civil War reenactors.

Leisch, Juanita. "Defining Historical Accuracy: Could, Would, Should Test." *Civil War Lady* 1, No. 1 (May-June 1991) pp.4-7.

Who They Were:
The "People of Color" During The Civil War

WHO THEY WERE

Fig. 8. SLAVES   Fig. 9. HOUSE SLAVES

Fig. 10. "FREE PEOPLE OF COLOR"   Fig. 11. MILITARY "PEOPLE OF COLOR"

Who They Were: The "People of Color" During the Civil War

During the years of the Civil War, 1861-1865, who were the "people of color"? They were black civilians whose ancestors had been brought unwillingly from Africa and were either slaves or "free people of color." For generations they had lived in the United States, yet they were neither considered nor treated as American citizens with the rights and privileges enjoyed by whites. Whether they suffered in bondage or were among the fortunate few considered free, laws restricting their lives were passed that cast them permanently into a low class. They were perceived as an inferior race of people. (They were not referred to as African-Americans, but as blacks, Africans, Negroes, Niggers, Colored, or "Persons of Color" in most historic records of the period.)

In America, the color of the skin mattered. The "free person of color" may have obtained that distinction in a number of ways. Slaves who fought in the American Revolution became free and from that beginning, many became the offspring or descendants of free parents. Others in bondage may have been manumitted by law; or they may have worked and purchased their freedom from a willing master, or freedom was purchased by another person. Others were freed in wills or were given freedom which was earned by giving some type of meritorious service. Children of free mothers were born free. The legal status of the mother determined the status of her children. Slave mothers bore slave children. The race of fathers was never considered. Many in bondage obtained their freedom by fleeing to northern states that no longer held slaves. They became abolitionists and worked for the freedom of others. As "free persons of color" in free states, they were not restricted as much as "free persons of color" in slave states.

Even though a person of color was legally "free" in a slave holding state, his status was so restricted by laws that he was barely freer than a slave. He was required to have a white guardian and carry a certificate of proof of his status; he was required to register each year, state his parentage, color, and special markings for identity and to pay special taxes. Failure to pay taxes resulted in fines. Other infractions of laws could cast him into slavery. Laws permitted "free persons of color" to be kept constantly under surveillance. They could not handle legal matters. They were considered as minors needing guardians or protectors. This was further evidence of whites' perception of black people as inferior beings.

With the beginning of the Civil War, interest in the freedom of all in bondage was foremost in the minds of slaves and "free people of color" in both northern and southern states. At that time, the lives of all people of color, whether bonded or free were affected.

A MEMBER OF A FREE BLACK FAMILY OF SALEM, MASSACHUSETTS

Fig. 12. Mrs. James Babcock, a Business Woman Baker

Mrs. Babcock is dressed in a plain colored soft silk dress with a fitted bodice and pagoda sleeves. White cotton undersleeves show near her hands. The dress front and sleeves have pleated trimming. A gold chain is attached to the waist. A pin connects the narrow white detachable collar. Her typical 1860s hair style has the center part and a braid across the top and hair softly curled over her ears. *Courtesy of Essex Peabody Institute (14-849)*

While those in slavery sneaked under the piazza or hid in trees to hear talk in the Big House by plantation owners about the beginning and progress of the war, they whispered in the cabins their hopes for freedom that the war might bring. At the same time, slaves were pressed into Confederate service as "body-servants" and went off to camp to continue what they had done all of their lives, serve their young masters. After the war, comments from soldiers gave great tribute to the loyalty of those men to the "southern cause" never mindful of the fact that their loyalty was to their masters around whom they had lived all of their lives. Yet deep within was the yearning for freedom that the war might bring. Others devised escape plans and left the squalor of the slave cabins to escape and join Union forces.

"Free People of Color" or *fpc*

"Free people of color" although described as "free" were forced to serve in the Confederacy. The Confederate Army used the labor of free blacks during the Civil War. In Virginia, a law required *all* free black men between the ages of 18 and 50 to work as laborers on fortifications for six months. They especially desired skilled laborers; however, white citizen complaints kept some skilled persons home in their communities. Even though free blacks were not inducted or mustered into the Confederate army, they had to abide by the law and report for work. If they did not, they were sentenced to death. They were paid for their work, $11.00 per month, so that they could support their families. (1, pp.205-206)

Officers in the Confederacy sought the manual and domestic labor of free blacks to release their soldiers to fight. Some free blacks tried to avoid having to obey the law by pretending to be slaves and by seeking employment in the cities as hotel workers, for example. However, if caught, they were punished.

What was life like for a "free person of color?" In a nut shell, the answer is "not much different from the life of a slave." Specific laws governed their every move.

In Henrico County, Virginia, a *fwc* (free woman of color) was caught living with a slave, probably her husband, for this she was whipped. The problem was, the slave did not have the permission of his master. People of color, although free, were not respected as free citizens by the ruling class. Their freedom was always threatened. If suspected as a run-away, a free black could be caught and instantly sold as a slave.

"Free people of color" living in states that held slaves in 1860 numbered approximately 251,000. More than anything else, these people had to walk a thin line daily to avoid being thrust into slavery. To be found guilty of any crime like stealing, would result in enslavement of the

"Free People of Color" or *fpc*

perpetrator. Men above the age of 21 had to pay taxes and if they became default, they were forced to join a road gang and receive ten cents a day. First and foremost though, was the law that required free Negroes to register. Courthouse clerks recorded each name, age, color, address, prominent skin markings, and how his/her freedom was obtained: whether by birth of a free mother, manumission by a will, or purchase by a free relative. Each person had to carry a "free paper" and could become sold as a slave if caught at any time without that paper. Two women in Virginia advertised in a newspaper that their "free papers" were lost and they would apply at the courthouse for replacements.

Laws restricted their movement: If a free Negro left the state of Virginia to get an education, he could not return; one law stated that once free, the person had to leave the state within a year, but the law was not always enforced and many remained in order to reside in close proximity to their enslaved relatives.

Free people of color purchased their slave relatives whenever possible, but the former master sometimes *did not* allow them to free their relatives so they became "slave owners" or, as in South Carolina, the law forbade free blacks from freeing their slaves. In other instances, the black slave owner could free his slaves at his will.

A *fpc* (free person of color) was not allowed to smoke in public or visit the train depot unless a white person accompanied him or her. Neither was he allowed to go into the city of Richmond without a certificate of good character from a justice of peace.

In the autobiography of Mary Livermore, a teacher from Boston who was hired to teach six Henderson children on a Virginia plantation in Mecklinburg County, she stated that "new clothing was ordered from stores in Richmond" for the Henderson's family Christmas celebration. This has implication for the clothing selected by reenactors in the roles of free people of color.

If free Negroes were not allowed to freely enter the city of Richmond to shop, even though some of them were marginally wealthy and possessed some education, they may not have dressed lavishly or elaborately in the styles of period ball gowns. (Few photographs are available to illustrate the clothing styles of free blacks in the ante-bellum period.) With all of the restrictions, it appears certain, or a reasonable assumption, that free blacks would have been less inclined to present or have elaborate social balls to attend. Free people of color lived in constant fear of being kidnapped and sold into slavery. In spite of that, they established schools and churches and organized benevolent societies.

One half of the property owners in one Virginia County among the free people of color were females. A few became wealthy. However, all were subjected to discriminating circumstances economically and socially. For example, laws forbade them from the ownership of grocery stores and cookhouses. However, some defied the law. No matter the circumstances, free blacks were never considered the equal of whites, and black men were never to be addressed as "gentlemen."

There were laws restricting the types of occupations for free blacks. However, documents give evidence that many worked as mechanics, coopers, carpenters, wheelwrights, bricklayers, stonemasons, seamstresses, barbers, cooks, bakers, blacksmiths and in other occupations. There were whites who relied upon their skilled labor, while others like slave owners who had contempt for free Negroes, resented their employment which they felt affected job opportunities for white people.

During the Civil War, the Confederacy attempted to restrict blacks from work in their trades by removing them from their communities and sending them to Confederate camps. Complaints from farmers and others who depended upon their labor changed the policy, thus enabling free blacks to remain at home to continue laboring as skilled artisans. During the war, white businesses hired free blacks and paid them wages in order to maintain their livelihood and success in business. As a result, many free Negroes became wealthy property owners and tax payers.

According to the research of the authors of the books in the bibliography following this chapter, restrictive laws governing the lives of free people of color were about the same as the laws of Virginia referred to in this chapter. In all southern states where the fortunate few free people of color were, they resided in separate communities. They lived apart from those still laboring under the yoke of slavery, who often included members of their own families.

Slaves: Field Hands and House Servants

During the first year of the Civil War, life went on as usual for slave field hands and house slave servants. On all plantations, field hands and house servants were intensely interested in knowing how the war would affect their lives. However, knowledge that the war was going on somewhere in the distance did not diminish their labor or the growth of weeds in the cotton, tobacco, or sugar cane fields. Neither were the chores less in the "Big House" for the house servants. However, the second and third years of the war brought noticeable changes. These changes came with the Federals or Union soldiers' invasion of the South as they marched by and through plantations. Many field hands and house servants left to follow the soldiers. Living conditions became difficult, not only for the slaves, but also for the slave owning families.

Labor Differences

A study of slave life during the ante-bellum period showed much variation in the lives of slaves on different plantations. In most instances, the lives of field hands were considerably harder than those of house slave servants. Long work hours in the sun and in all kinds of weather for either six or seven days a week was typical for field hands. Some worked on a task system. A certain amount of work was assigned each day and when the task was completed, the slave was finished for the day. Otherwise, field laborers worked from before sunrise until darkness with only a break for a meal. Either a central kitchen for food preparation was provided for the field hands or they used individual fireplaces in their cabins. Evening meals were prepared either in the cabins or in the general slave kitchen. Women, too old for field work, served as nurses to keep small children while their parents worked in the fields.

The quarters or houses of those who worked in the slave master's house were better constructed and located closer to the Big House than the slave quarters of field hands whose cabins were located a distance away. House servants often slept inside the master's house on the floor either within or outside bedroom doors or on the kitchen floor within a nearby building. They were on call for service at any time, day or night. Field hands may not have been allowed in the yard of the Big House unless summoned there.

House servants were better clothed and fed than field workers. Clothing was distributed twice each year and most slaves had a minimum of two changes of clothing. House servants received old faded hand-me down clothing made in more attractive styles than the coarse fabric made into field-hand slave clothing.

Some male slaves were selected for training in building trades and became skilled artisans. Even though blacks were considered an inferior race, incapable of independent living or military service and by law were denied the privilege of learning to read and write, records exist that dispute those assumptions. Young slaves were "hired out" to be trained in various skills as carpenters, blacksmiths, brick masons, wheelwrights, cabinet makers, coopers (builders of barrels), seamstresses, boot and shoemakers, and in numerous other skills as needed. All work on plantations was done by slaves under the watchful eyes of overseers.

During the war, many skilled slaves were pressed into service for the Confederacy. The same as before the war, masters received pay for their service.

The provision of slave clothing and shoes for a large plantation was a great responsibility. It was made more difficult during the war years after the blockade of southern ports because clothing and other goods from northern mills were no longer available. Spinning wheels and weaving machines were returned to use by plantation mistresses for their own family's clothing and for the master's slaves. But most of the spinning and weaving was done by slaves. Slave mistresses cut the cloth for garments, taught and supervised the sewing by the slave women. The head house slave, designated as "mammy," may have shared in the teaching and supervision of slave women who became skilled in fancy needlework: knitting, lace making, tatting, knitting, crocheting and quilt making.

Slave boot and shoemakers made those items on the plantations. The following describes one method used: the upper parts of shoes were made from tanned cow hides, while the soles were made from soft wood and tacked to the upper parts by slave blacksmiths. An iron rim was placed around each shoe for the attachment. Only adult slaves received shoes once per year.

The need to feed the Confederate army forced a change in the products grown in the fields. The Confederacy urged planters to diminish their cotton production and instead, grow more food stuffs. With more food available, the diet of field slaves was improved.

During the war years, the most noticeable change on slave plantations was the conduct of slave holders and the behavior of their slaves. When the call went out to build armies to fight for the Confederate cause, white men readily left their homes to serve. With fewer overseers left and persons to keep vigil at night patrolling the premises to keep runaways from escaping, a grave situation became apparent. This situation caused fear of slave uprisings among slave holders. As slaves began to leave to join the Union troops who came within the vicinity of the plantations, slave holders had that problem as a concern. With the absence of so many whites, some slaves became insubordinate, refused to work, refused to submit to punishment and roamed around at night without written permission. Plantation mistresses, left to supervise, were in the precarious position of not knowing what to do when whippings administered by neighbors or others, did not remedy the situation. Some decided to be content with whatever work the slaves did.(2, p.76)

Slaves

As a result, plantation owners held town meetings to decide how to rigidly control their human property. They compelled sixteen-and seventeen-year-old boys and men too old for military service, to serve as patrollers or "pattyrollers," the name given to these guards by the slaves. Laws were passed to further control the movement of slaves. For example, it became unlawful for a slave to use a small boat alone. High crimes punishable with death by hanging was eminent when a slave showed any intention of defecting to the Union, or was caught within a plot of insurrection. Slave owners closely observed slave behavior as the war commenced.

Field hands became suspect relative to their loyalty. The most loyal to their owners were those who had developed close ties because of kind treatment. Especially loyal were those who became "body servants" to their young masters in Confederate camps. Next in loyalty were the house servants and the black drivers or foremen. The field hands or those who were not closely associated with the slave master's family were less likely to be the ones to hide the slave master and his family whenever Union forces were approaching. In fact, they often aided the Federals or Union soldiers in whatever ways they could.

Slaves with close ties seldom betrayed the trust placed in them by their owners. When they were asked to keep and hide large sums of money, silver or valuables in the event of Union raids on the premises, they, having become servile in nature and obedient to following orders, did as they were told without hesitation. They buried valuables, hid them upon themselves or sewed them into bed mattresses in their cabins. The items were always returned. On the other hand, field hands aided the Union soldiers in locating the valuables.

Instances of positive loyalty by house servants were the exceptions rather than the common reaction of the majority of slaves. House servants were fewer in number than field workers in the slave population.

During and after the war, the conduct of slaves on numerous plantations following the invasion of Union troops was reported in letters and newspapers like the *Southern Recorder*. The Union soldiers who raided the plantation mansions influenced the slaves, especially the field hands. Loud shouts, dancing, and joyful hoopla reined as they heard the news of their freedom. They took quick possession of the fleeing slave master's property. They either drove off the overseer or locked him up if he had not escaped as the Union soldiers came near. The Yankees told the slaves that "every thing was theirs." The slaves quit work and celebrated by taking all that they desired of household furnishings, "beds, carpets, and everything"(2,p.78) and completely destroyed the master's house. Similar happenings occurred on plantations in several southern states wherever the Yankees took over the plantations.

Although all were in bondage, the field hands and house servants, and both subjected to follow orders of the slave masters and mistresses, the nature of their conduct during the war depended upon their treatment *before* the war. The degrees of extreme kindness or extreme cruelty were evidenced by the amount of social life permitted on the plantations. Whether slave masters allowed dancing, weddings, quilting parties and corn shuckings determined one way of judging treatment of slave property.

Weddings, Quilting Parties and Corn Shuckings

Tempe Herndon, a house servant, wore a formal wedding gown with a veil, both made by her slave mistress. She had a wedding cake for the big eating following the ceremony for all of the slaves on the plantation. In contrast, one field slave reported that she was married "while standing behind a plow in the field." Some wedding ceremonies consisted of a few scripture verses read from the Bible by the slave master and the simple "jumping over the broom" to seal the unspoken vows. When the regular wedding ceremony was read, the part about "until death do us part" was omitted. No slave marriages were legal and slaves had the understanding that the couple could be separated by sale at any time by the wishes of the slave master. Permission for a marriage union was required from the slave master of both parties before one could take place. One implication of disregard for the human dignity of slaves as people with human feelings was apparent when the slave master forced a marriage partnership by selecting the partners himself, completely disregarding the wishes of the man or woman.

Whether social gatherings were allowed suggests a way of measuring the quality of life for those in bondage. Quilting parties were sometimes arranged by the slave holding family. Slave women gathered in one cabin in the evening to sew on quilts for their families and the master's family. Men and children attended. It was a fun time for gossiping, storytelling, courting and eating. Food was either furnished or unfurnished by the plantation mistress. When unfurnished, the house servant cooks sneaked food to them. When quilting parties or Saturday evening dancing was never allowed, this lack of social outlets indicated a disregard for this need of escape from their unpaid labor.

Corn shuckings provided a time for slaves from surrounding plantations to get together for fun while shucking huge piles of corn. At these gatherings, relatives and friends were present to fellowship with each other. The host plantation slaves prepared the food for all to enjoy. These slave gatherings indicated some kindness in the slave master.

Of course, the greatest influence which controlled the conduct of all slaves during the Civil War years, whether they labored in the fields or in the Big House, was the overall treatment of slaves as human beings. Were they clothed and fed well? Were there forced family separations, or

The Desolate Home
Fig. 13. Southern plantation households became desolate when husbands, sons and overseers left to fight for the Confederacy. Some household servants remain faithful, while others and field workers became difficult for plantation wives to manage. *Library of Congress-USZ62-37846.*

constant cruel and severe punishments given? Even with kind and considerate masters, freedom was still a sincere desire of both field hands and house servants. Those in bondage saw the war as the possible answer to their daily prayers for deliverance. One slave woman uttered each time that she heard the sound of a cannon blast, "Ride on King Jesus."

---

1. Jordan, Ervin L. <u>Black Confederates and Afro Yankees in Civil War Virginia.</u> Charlottesville: Univ. of VA. 1995. "
    Free black men were also subject to conscription as laborers for saltpeter and munitions work but were permitted to hire themselves out rather than being drafted...Those between the ages of eighteen and fifty were required to report to Confederate fortifications for military labor. Promised fair compensation, rations, living quarters, and medical care, these men by law, were not to be detained for more than 180 days. Failure to report could result in the death penalty under the articles of war on the charges of desertion and disobedience, despite the fact that they were civilians." pp.205-206

2. Wiley, Bell Irvin. <u>Southern Negroes, 1861-1865.</u> Baton Rouge: Louisiana State Univ., 1938. Chapter IV "Conduct."

Bibliography

These titles give an informative study of "free people of color:" how they lived and rendered service in the Civil War and an explanation of how slaves on southern plantations were affected by the war.

Berlin, Slaves Without Masters, The Free Negro in The Ante-Bellum South. NY: New York Press, 1974
    A well-researched and documented description of the lives and times of "free people of color." Chapter titles include: "The Origin of the Free Negro Caste," "The Sources of Free Negro Identity," and "The Free Negro Community."

Hodges, Willis Augustus. Free Man of Color, The Autobiography of Willis Augustus Hodges.+ Edited by Willard B. Gatewood, Jr. Knoxville: Univ. of Tennessee Press, 1962.
    Hodges, a free black born in Virginia in 1815, helps readers view the struggles of blacks in the ante-bellum South through his eyes.

Johnson, Michael P. and James L. Roark. Black Masters, A Free Family of Color in the Old South, NY: W.W. Norton & Co., 1984.
    The authors describe the living conditions and laws governing "free people of color" in South Carolina. They researched and documented the life story of April Ellison, a slave who was trained as an apprentice to become a gin maker. He later purchased his freedom and that of his family. April changed his slave name to William and established a successful business as a builder and repairer of gins. He became very wealthy and was the owner of 63 slaves before his death at the beginning of the Civil War. His family, as free people, occupied a mansion once owned by a governor of South Carolina. The authors describe the continuous, yet unsuccessful efforts of South Carolina Congressmen to enslave all of the state's free people of color. At each time, some white friends supporters came to their defense.

Jordan, Ervin L. Jr. Black Confederates and Afro-Yankees in Civil War Virginia. Charlottesville, VA: University of Virginia, 1995.
    This book is written from a point of view that may spark controversy. To obtain a balanced view of black participation in the Civil War, the published research of other authors should be consulted, including specifically Berlin and Quarles.
    Jordan describes the laws governing living conditions of free people and their non-combat roles in Confederate units during the Civil War. Virginia and Maryland had the largest population of free Negroes.

Koger, Larry. Black Slave Owners, Free Black Slave Masters in South Carolina, 1790-1860. Columbia, SC: Univ. of South Carolina Press, 1995.
    The author's quest to learn who black slave masters were and why free African-Americans owned slaves, led him to research, write, and publish his book. Koger's publication answers those questions. Chapter titles include: "From Slavery to Freedom to Slave ownership;" "Free Black Artisans: A Need for Labor;" and "Buying My Chidrum from Ole Massa."

Quarles, Benjamin. The Negro In The Civil War. Boston: Little, Brown & Co., 1969.
    Quarles presents a documented study of the vital role played by Negroes in the Civil War as soldiers, scouts, spies, nurses, abolitionists and workers on the Underground Railroad.

Wiley, Bell Irvin. Southern Negroes, 1861-1865. N.Y.: Random House, 1938.
    The author presents a documented account of life of Southern Negroes during the Civil War and in their transition from slavery to freedom.

SLAVE REMOVAL

Fig. 14. LEAVING CHARLESTON ON THE CITY BEING BOMBARDED.

Chapter 2
Life on Southern Plantations During the Civil War Years, 1861-1865

By the time the Civil War began, millions of black slave men, women, and children on southern plantations comprised several generations removed from their original homeland of Africa. Even so, the distant beat and rhythms of drums continued to echo in the slave songs which carried their hopes and dreams for freedom. Slaves learned about the coming of the war through various means: by crawling under the "Big House" or from a perch on tree limbs, as masters and guests chatted on the piazzas after supper; and from house servants who served the meals. On almost every plantation, according to reports from "slave narratives,"[1] there was at least one slave who had somehow learned to read. This person met the slave on the road from town as he returned with newspapers. The papers were read aloud before the carrier reached the master's house. The carrier also stood around and listened to bystanders as they discussed news about the forthcoming war. As the conflict progressed, these tactics continued to help the slaves keep pace with war-filled events. In the war's earliest stages, those in bondage instinctively felt that the war was about them and slavery.

Stated broadly in southern newspapers, at family gatherings, and wherever southern planters talked was the belief: "this is a white man's war" and it will soon end with a Confederate victory.

The Master-Slave Relationship

The master-slave relationship changed as slaves observed the changing moods of their owners when sons left home for Confederate service. Fears of emancipation of their slaves brought out the worse traits in some slave holders. Even those who were formerly kind changed their behavior. The slaves knew from life experiences how to keep within their "place" and voice no understanding of the coming conflict. But within the isolation of the slave quarters, they soon whispered their beliefs that somehow the frustrations and tensions seen in the "Big House" by their "white folks" had much to do with them. (*Big House* was the slaves' name for their slave master's home.)

As the war commenced, changes came in other ways. Food and clothing became scarce. Anger and bitterness rose in slaves as they saw the food they had raised given to support Confederate troops or kept to sustain families in the Big House. With a decrease in an already meager diet, undernourished bodies suffered even more from ill health as long hours of unpaid labor never diminished. Food rations typically included three pounds of bacon or pork and three quarts of cornmeal a week per person supplemented with vegetables grown in personal vegetable plots located near their cabins.

The Confederate and Union States

Even before Abraham Lincoln, the newly-elected President, took the oath at his inauguration, South Carolina seceded from the Union. Many feared during the 1860 election campaign that if Lincoln won, he would use his executive powers to free the slaves. Other slave holding states soon followed South Carolina and seceded from the Union. Eleven states comprised the Confederacy: Alabama, Arkansas, Florida, Georgia, Louisiana, Mississippi, North Carolina, South Carolina, Tennessee, Texas and Virginia. Delegates chose Jefferson Davis as their President and Richmond, Virginia as the Confederate capitol.

The remaining twenty-three states formed the Union: California, Connecticut, Delaware, Illinois, Indiana, Iowa, Kansas, Kentucky; Maine, Maryland, Massachusetts, Michigan, Minnesota, Missouri, New Hampshire, New Jersey, New York, Ohio, Oregon, Pennsylvania, Rhode Island, Vermont and Wisconsin. The territories of Colorado, Dakota, Nebraska, Nevada, New Mexico, Utah, and Washington also fought on the Union side.(2, p.617)

Following the Confederate attack on Fort Sumter April 12, 1861, Lincoln declared that something had to be done to quell the rebels. Lincoln issued a call for troops and ordered a blockade of the South. Life for blacks did not go on as usual in the North or South. Abolitionists in the North fashioned a new focus having to decide how they would continue their service. Secret hiding places that once sheltered escaping slaves, now hid spies or Union soldiers escaping capture. Abolitionists addressed without ceasing the issue of slavery and pressed support for emancipation. Escaped blacks, formerly in bondage, rushed to give military service but were turned away.

A small number of free blacks living in areas of the South apart from their bonded fellowmen voiced sentiments in favor of the Confederates. They, like William Ellison, wanted to hold on to their material possessions. Ellison, apprenticed while a slave by his master, had acquired skills in building cotton gins. He purchased his freedom and that of his wife and family. As a free black, he established a financially successful business of building and repairing cotton gins; he owned slaves and amassed a fortune. As a slave in Fairfield District, South Carolina, Williams changed his slave name from *April* to William.[3]

After the war began, he, like most cotton planters, ceased the production of cotton and began to grow food stuffs for the Confederate army. Ellison and his family had been fortunate enough to acquire property and were most interested in holding on to their investments.[3] A number equal to a hand count of free blacks in South Carolina volunteered to serve in the Confederate military. However, military records do not show actual enlistments. The majority of free blacks favored the Union cause.

Impressment of Slaves

Ordered from their quarters on southern plantations, black male slaves armed with spades, shovels, and other working tools, were pressed into non-combat Confederate military service. Impressment of slaves became a widespread practice. Slaves were viewed as a needed source of manpower in the military for domestic labor: cooking, washing, ironing, building fortifications, digging trenches, cutting down trees for building earthworks, and other back-breaking tasks to release the Confederate soldiers with arms to fight. Skilled slave carpenters and brick masons were in the lot. For the labor of their human property, slave masters received thirty dollars per month.(4,p.37)

Slave masters insisted that their slaves be kept behind the front lines in battles. They were fearful of losing their financial value if their slaves were killed. If death occurred, slave masters expected to be paid the "value" of the deceased slave. After the war, reports from slaves who labored in Confederate camps indicated that the labor was hard, and they often were not fed well nor did they receive adequate medical attention. Blacks were not considered "fit" for the military. Southerners were wary about arming slaves as they feared the weapons would be turned towards them or the slaves would cross over to the Union. The role of the slave remained, as it always had, servile in complete obedience with punishment by whipping or even death in extreme cases.

Other black men were present in Confederate camps serving as "body servants" to their young masters. As domestic house servants, they had grown up serving them all of their lives. In every assigned task, the slaves continued to work in menial roles. Soldiers with body servants enjoyed with strident and boastful pride, special attention from their fellow comrades as they represented southern planter aristocracy. With body servants to attend their personal needs, they were the envy of other soldiers from the non-slave holding class.

Contrary to published accounts, the service of body servants was not given as "loyal patriotism to the cause of the southerners." When told to go, the slaves, compelled to follow their owners' orders, went to military camps. While in camp, they remained "slaves" and in that position, they were forced to obey their masters no matter where they were. They were sometimes given uniforms and photographed with their slave masters, turned Confederate soldiers. To fail to obey, or show any signs of possible non-compliance, or even the slightest insinuation that they favored a Union victory, led to suffering from immediate punishment. However, reports to Union officers from blacks who slipped into their lines, indicated that they were formerly body servants and deserters from Confederate camps. They had escaped to the Union side while in battle. Then as body servants (deserters) they became informants or spies for the Union. However, many body servants remained with their Confederate soldier slave masters throughout the war. Confederate soldier reports following the war praised the service of body servants and even honored their service with awards in memorial ceremonies.

During the final months of the war, repeated debates were held in the Confederate Congress on the topic of whether to enlist slaves officially. Some Confederate officers expressed willingness to arm and train slaves, while others objected. However, because of constant complaints from slave masters about the impressment of their slaves, the Confederate War Department decided to press *free* blacks into military service in non-combat roles. Laws were passed and free blacks were pressed into Confederate service to build fortifications. Some Confederate officers did arrange for some free blacks to be uniformed to fight; however, historians who have researched the subject, report no findings of *authentic* Confederate enlistment of black troops in official Confederate military records. The Civil War ended one month before the final decision was made to enlist blacks for the Confederacy. (See Appendix D, Letter of J. H. Stringfellow to President Jefferson Davis.)

The Plantation Mistress

With the blockade in southern ports, came a shortage in the supply of clothing and numerous other items. Plantation mistresses returned to homespun fabric-making to fulfill their need for clothing. They resented the wearing of clothing with the resemblance of osnaburg or "nigger cloth" as they called it. Faded, worn-out dresses were turned under-side out to extend their use. When the war first began, silk dresses were made into battle flags and banners.

Fear and Anxiety in the "Big House"

When masters and their sons went off to join the Confederates, wives and daughters were left to manage their slaves. They felt unprepared for this new responsibility. They expressed in journals and diaries fear of personal safety from overseers and fear of slave uprisings. The women felt helpless with so many blacks around them and few white men for security. They wrote letters to their husbands filled with accounts of mistrust and disobedience of slaves to their orders. Wives requested state governors to "leave at least one white man for a specified number of slaves on each plantation." The wives observed work stoppages in the fields and slaves leaving the premises without getting the required "written permission." They turned to neighbors and white men from town to inflict punishment upon disobedient and unruly slaves.

Recordings in diaries, journals, letters and newspapers of the Civil War era revealed the overwhelming affect of the war upon living conditions of those in bondage and those in the Big House. Leon F. Litwack's research into slave testimonies recount quotes of slaves who told of their plantation life experiences during the Civil War in the beginning chapters of his book titled, <u>Been In The Storm So Long, The Aftermath of Slavery.</u> (NY: Random, 1979).

Experiences ranged from both extremes. Some slaves were treated with more kindness in hopes of discouraging them from running away to Union camps. On the other hand, when news of a Confederate-loss-son in battle reached home, as mothers mourned, fathers took revenge on the backs of slaves in a frenzy of cussed words and the sound of the whip while lambasting the slaves as the cause of all the trouble. Likewise, recorded in slave narratives are reports of whippings on slave wives by slave masters when they learned that slave husbands and sons had escaped to Union lines. (See Appendix C)

It was an unusual sight for slaves to witness emotional upheaval in those who had, all of their lives, wielded relentless power and control over them. Even though attempts were made to shield their slaves from witnessing the anguish and anxiety brought on by the war, their efforts were in vain. The slaves had years of experience in interpreting facial expressions and guarded behavior. Those in bondage were careful to conceal their true feelings about the war.

Slaves were well acquainted with sadness and grief from forced family separations and whippings resulting in deaths of loved ones. Yet, many shed tears with the master's family when they suffered personal losses of loved ones in the war. When their wounded sons returned home maimed with missing legs and arms, slaves, no doubt, experienced mingled emotions in the presence of their owners. After all, many had grown up playing with their masters' children and slave mothers had even nursed them as babies.

Fears of Runaways

Masters and mistresses used all sorts of strategies to hold on to their "human property." The approaching Union soldiers were described as having "horns and tails and they will kill you," the slaves were told. Preposterous and terrifying tales were told to the slaves on how they would be cruelly treated by the Yankees in blue (Union soldiers) if they were caught. They "kill black children, even roasted and ate them." Slaves were told to run and hide in the woods and to lie if questioned about the whereabouts of household valuables, like jewelry, money, and silverware. If asked whether or not they were fed, clothed and treated well, their responses were to be always "good" regardless of whether or not there was any resemblance of truth. If asked if they wanted to be free, the slaves were directed to say "No." The reaction of the slaves to the dire predictions and warnings about the Yankee soldiers was disbelief. They had no reasons to have any more faith and confidence in the words of those who owned them than before.

Contrabands of War

As soon as those in bondage learned that following the Union soldiers freed them from slavery, they left the plantations in droves. During the beginning months of the war, fugitives were returned to the plantations, but when General Benjamin Butler kept the first ones who came under his direct command, he labeled them "Contrabands of War." The tide turned. The news was like swift-spreading like wild fire. Federal legislation in 1862 barred Union officers from returning the slaves and stated that escaped slaves would be considered free. (4, p.52)

However, in published recorded incidents, when some slaves left, those remaining were questioned about their intentions. Slaves had learned to show feelings of indifference in the presence of whites and made verbal promises to remain on the plantations. But at the same time, if the slightest opportunity arrived enticing them to a means of escape, they took it. Yankee soldiers in the vicinity of the plantation or passing by gave them that long-sought opportunity. Without hesitation, entire families fled, often with only the clothes on their backs. As they entered Union lines, they became free.

Mistresses were baffled when their most esteemed and trusted "house servants" sneaked away in the dark of night to escape to Union lines. With house servants who had grown up in the family and bonded well with the family, a close relationship had developed. The whites eventually came to understand that those in bondage desired their freedom whether they had been treated well or not.

The slaves were equally stunned and puzzled when they saw their owners run to hide from the approaching Yankees as they neared the plantations. To see "white folks" afraid of other "white folks" was an entirely new, bewildering experience. The slaves worked and carried on their lives in the usual manner. They appeared "calm and their emotions discreetly hidden, seemingly unaffected by discussions about the war in their presence," was the observation of mistresses in their letters. Before their "white folks," (slave owners) they were careful not to show any appearance of concern about the war or the turmoil in the master's household. When the Yankees were sighted, some slaves showed their loyalty by helping to hide the master and his family, then immediately fled with his family, leaving the plantation with the Yankees. Slaves sneaked away on foot, on horseback or in the slave master's wagons.

One fugitive told a Union officer about her experience as a house servant. She and her son were fleeing to Union lines while being pursued by her slave master's son. He shot at them both. The mother escaped but her son was hit and later died. The mother lamented, "I nursed him at my own breasts along with my son. They were the same age. My slave mistress had her daughter sit and watch me to make sure that her baby son received his due of milk. Now my son is dead, his life taken. Two years ago, my husband and two of my children were sold away from me."

Some slaves expressed faithfulness to their "white folks" and remained with them. They hid and kept secret their food and precious valuables. Body servants mourned the loss of their fallen young masters, and other slaves joined in mourning when the news reached the plantation. Slaves on thousands of plantations and farms were recipients of varying degrees of kindness, some were treated with less cruelty than others, but all desired freedom.

Slave Removal

One strategy used by many slave owners to hold on to their property was removal to other states. From Mississippi and Georgia, for example, observers saw over-stuffed wagons spilling over with household goods and people going to Texas on crowded roads. Young slave children trudged along barefoot besides parents for many miles. Death came to some along the way. See Fig 14, p. 20.)

Once runaway slaves or contrabands slipped into Union camps, they were brought before the officers and questioned. Their knowledge of the roads, waterways and terrain left behind enabled them to become excellent sources of information to the Union. Some gave information on Confederate campsites, troop movements, estimates of their number, the location of their ammunition and supplies. Some contrabands became spies. Posed as body servants, they slipped back into Confederate camps and became the eyes and ears for the Union as they gathered useful dependable information. They risked their lives to assist the Union. Had they been caught, severe punishment would have resulted: death by hanging.

Plantation slaves assisted Union soldiers in spite of the tales told them by their "white folks." When possible, they helped captured soldiers to escape. Women fugitives became cooks and washerwomen in Union camps and became assistants in hospitals. The men helped to build fortifications and to forage for food.

These black civilians, called fugitives or contrabands of war, served the Union well. Their service in non-combat roles was an important and significant contribution to Union victory. Their labor freed the soldiers with guns to fight. All of their efforts demonstrated a deep craving to be free. They had perceived the war as their pathway to freedom and, as it turned out, it was.

Southern Plantations

As a people bound by the confines of the plantation, who lived for generations under the stress, strains and humiliating circumstances of human bondage, with denial of a privileged education and with every aspect of their lives completely controlled and directed, black people in bondage had learned to bow down, become docile, humble, and passive. They feigned happiness in their demeanor. Deceptive "joy" expressed in slave songs and dancing hid their true meanings. They had trained themselves in the fine art of survival. Singing and dancing were their tools.

They had learned well how to disguise their true selves. To those who towered over them, they presented only a *deceptive face* of happiness and contentment. But deep within was a steadfast yearning. With the earliest news of the conflict, they perceived it to be about them and the possibility of freedom.

And so they served during the Civil war to secure that freedom. They gave valuable aid to the Union as dependable informants; as foragers for food and the preparation of it; as washerwomen to keep their uniforms clean; as teamsters and skilled laborers in the building of fortifications; as guides to lead lost soldiers back to their units; as friends to those captured in Confederate prisons and as spies for the Union officers. They rendered faithful, valued service in essential non-combat roles. By so doing, they forged the fight for their freedom and won.

Well worth remembering:

Reenactors in the low garb of slave clothing,
Lift in honor and high esteem,
Deserved praise for the sacrificial service
Of those fugitive freedom fighters who:
Suffered through the trials of slavery,
Rendered non-combat military service as "Contrabands of War,"
To earn their freedom and keep this country a nation.

---

1. In the 1930s, about 2000 former slaves were interviewed in a Federal Writer's Project. These published interviews are referred to as "Slave Narratives."

2. World Book Encyclopedia, 1991 edition, v.4.

3. Johnson, Michael P. and James L. Roark. Black Masters, A Free Family of Color in the Old South. NY: W.W. Norton & Co., 1984.

4. Litwack, Leon F. Been In The Storm So Long, The Aftermath of Slavery. NY: Random House, 1979.

Bibliography
Slavery and Plantation Life

These titles answer the question: What was life like for a slave? Detailed descriptions of work schedules and illustrations of authentic housing and clothing are included.

Bennett, Lerone, Jr. <u>Before the Mayflower, A History of Black America, The Classic Account of the Struggles and Triumphs of Black Americans.</u> NY: Penguin Bks.,1982.
    Bennett describes the Black family in the slave community, slave artisans, clothing, children, daily routine and countless other aspects of African- American history from slavery through the Civil Rights Movement.

Bial, Raymond. <u>The Strength of These Arms, Life in the Slave Quarters.</u> Boston: Houghton Mifflin Co., 1997.
    Includes numerous photographs and an easy-to read text.

Erickson, Paul. <u>Daily Life on a Southern Plantation, 1853.</u> NY: Dutton, Lodestar Bks., 1997.
    Includes authentic photographs of slave dwelling places, called "quarters" and the plantation owners' residence, (the Big House), storage houses, cookware, household furnishings, work tools, etc.

Fox-Genovese, Elizabeth. <u>Within the Plantation Household, Black and White Women of the Old South.</u> Chapel Hill, NC: University of North Carolina Press, 1988.
    Two chapters cover in detail facts about plantation life: "The View from the Big House" and "Between Big House and Slave Community." Two chapters discuss women's attitudes towards slavery: those who opposed slavery and those who did not.

Franklin, John Hope and Loren Schweninger. <u>Runaway Slaves, Rebels on The Plantation.</u> NY: Oxford University Press, 1999.
    Chapter titles: "The Plantation Household," "Backward Into Bondage"

Genovese, Eugene D. <u>Roll Jordan Roll, The World the Slaves Made</u>. NY: Vintage Bks., 1976.
    Chapter titles: "Life in the Big House," "Men of Skill," "Free Negroes" and "Clothes Make the Man and Woman." As the title suggests, the author describes all aspects in great detail about the plantation life of slaves.

Gutman, Herbert. <u>The Black Family in Slavery and Freedom, 1750-1925.</u> NY: Vintage Bks., 1976.
    Documented descriptions in great detail with charts and graphs depicting facts about Black family life in the years 1750-1925. A discussion of slave naming practices is included. This book will provide many hours of absorbed reading.

Johnson, Michael P. and James L. Roark. <u>Black Masters, A Free Family of Color in the Old South.</u> NY: W. W. Norton & Co., 1984.
    The factual story of William Ellison and family is given with documented details.

Bibliography
Slavery and Plantation Life

Litwack, Leon F. <u>Been In The Storm So Long., The Aftermath of Slavery.</u> NY: Random House, 1979.

    Litwack describes in vivid detail: how the Civil War vastly affected the lives of slaves and "white folks" on Southern plantations during the Civil War; the ever changing moods of the slave masters and mistresses as the war progressed and freedom of their slaves became eminent; how many slaves escaped to the Union lines; and the often brutal treatment meted upon slaves when knowledge of the masters' sons killed in action reached home. This is an important title, most deserving of being read.

Prather, <u>From Slave to Statesman, Legacy of Joshua Houston, Servant to Sam Houston.</u> Denton, TX: Univ. of North Texas Press, 1993.

    A researched biography of a slave, the loyal servant of Sam Houston and his family. Joshua is an example of many slaves who were extremely skilled as a carpenter, blacksmith and in numerous other skills.

Thomas, Velma Maia. <u>Lest We Forget, The Passage from Africa to Slavery and Emancipation.</u> NY.: Crown, 1997.

    A three-dimensional interactive book with photographs and documents. In this unique book, readers see and handle authentic copies of documents from the slavery era. Thomas' book makes an excellent addition to school library collections.

What They Did: The "People of Color" During The Civil War

Susie King Taylor.

WOODEN BUCKET

JOEL V. FEARS, SR.

JOEL V. FEARS, JR.

SKILLED CRAFTSMEN

Fig. 16. Father and son reenactors, Joel V. Fears, Sr. and Jr., are portrayed working as a cooper (maker of wooden buckets, tubs and barrels) and a cabinet maker. These are two of the various skills practiced by both slaves and "free people of color" before and during the Civil War. Slave artisans were often "hired out." However, the slave master received their earnings. Willing masters allowed a portion of the earnings to be kept by the slaves. Some slaves were sometimes fortunate enough to save enough funds to purchase their freedom. Free blacks labored in towns in various skilled areas.

Fig. 15. *On preceding page*, Susie King Taylor, Nurse. LC-USZ61-1863
(See also p.51.)

Chapter 3
Civilian "People of Color" Who Served in Non-Combat Roles

So often we read, "Blacks performed menial tasks for the soldiers in the Union Army during the Civil War. They dug trenches, cut down trees, built fortifications, washed uniforms, and cooked food." The words go on and on describing domestic tasks. But, whether soldier or servant, each had to have food and footwear.

Food and footwear, a soldier could neither function well nor venture far without either. Cooking was a menial task, domestic in nature. But here is a fact: a cook today in a fine restaurant is a *chef*; in today's army, he is the *mess sergeant* who orders the food and plans the meals as part of his supervisory duties; but he is first and foremost, a *cook*. In the navy, he is the *ship's cook* who works in the vessel's galley. No matter where he is, the quality of the cook's life and lives of his comrades *depend* upon the quality and availability of the food he prepares. The black hands of cooks were needed as much as firearms in the hands of infantry soldiers, or guns in the hands of gunners on Union gun boats, or the hands of artillery men loading huge cannons on Civil War battlefields. Reenactors as *cooks* honor their life-preserving service to the Union.

An ad for a commercial product featured a child saying, "Momma used Shake and Bake, and I helped." Likewise, a fact about the Civil War may be stated, *The Union won the war and civilian "people of color" helped.*

At Civil War battle reenactments, those civilian people, whether their identity is known or unknown by name, are characters deserving of living history interpretation. Historians credited black soldiers for their contribution to Union victory, but the roles assumed by black civilians during the war have not received adequate recognition in written works about the War Between the States.

Civilians served during the Civil War in important roles as recruiters, nurses, scouts, guides, spies, teamsters, wheelwrights, wagon masters, washerwomen, draymen, and cooks. As soon as the first guns were fired, fugitive slaves flocked to Union lines. In modern terms, they were *support personnel,* although unidentified with that descriptive distinction at that time.

As the Federal soldiers invaded Confederate territory, soldiers were forced to feed off the land. Former slaves were foragers of food and supplies. They "built forts and bridges; brought in boatloads of pine wood for army hospitals; baled cotton to be used for protection on gun boats; stripped corn fields; corralled horses and mules; rounded up pigs and cows; dug for potatoes;

climbed for fruit"(1, p.96) and with their spades, shovels, and pick axes, labored long hard hours to build earthworks and breastworks.

It is true, the Emancipation Proclamation proclaimed freedom for those held in bondage in the states in rebellion against the Union; and after the war, legal words in the 13th Amendment declared freedom for *all* in bondage--but the labor of those fugitive slaves as contrabands *earned* that freedom. Not shame, only gratitude, respect, and pride form an invisible badge of honor displayed by reenactors in slave attire.

Evidence exists in published works about the Civil War service of known people like Frederick Douglass, Harriet Tubman, Susie King Taylor, Elizabeth Bowser, Charlotte Forten, Elizabeth Keckley, and Sojourner Truth. However, there were multitudes of unnamed persons in the *slave population* and within the throngs of *"free people of color"* who served but can only be written about in general statements. The people in both groups, although with no specific roles, were citizens who lived during the years of the Civil War and who should be represented at reenactments in order to form the *complete* picture of the population during the Civil War era. Even though those two groups may not have been perceived by many as United States *citizens* who possessed and exercised the rights and privileges of citizens; yet, they were inhabitants who were not serving in the military; therefore, they were civilians.

Choices For Reenactment Roles

Outstanding characters, as well as individuals unknown by name, should be considered for reenactment roles in living history events to give recognition to "people of color." Research in libraries, archives, museums and other research centers are the places to look for biographical information about the persons whose lives will be interpreted.

Abolitionist

A reenactor may select the role of an *abolitionist* as a "free person of color" (fpc) who lived in a free state. When the war began, the "fpc" who lived in the northern states continued to aid fugitive slaves fleeing the slave states. But as the war progressed, they began actively recruiting black men to join the Union forces. Frederick Douglass was one of the most active recruiters. He and Sojourner Truth crusaded for black troops, not only to give them pride in their efforts to end slavery, but also to provide strong able-bodied men to assure a Union victory. A reenactor in the role of a *fpc* would dress appropriately as free people did during the 1860s. He or she would need to read about them in order to speak freely at reenactments about what the abolitionists did during the Civil War.

Skilled Craftsmen and Artisans

A large number of fugitive slaves were also skilled laborers. Male slaves had acquired specialized skills as blacksmiths, carpenters, coopers, cabinet makers, machinists, brick masons, tailors, boot and shoemakers. In addition to those were: milliners, tanners, upholsters, gunsmiths, millwrights, saddle makers, butchers and bookbinders. Others: manned river barges; built ornamental ironworks; worked as engineers in sawmills; while others repaired steam engines. The aforementioned occupations were listed on an 1848 South Carolina "Census of Manual Occupations." On very large plantations, the many skills of slaves created an independent community.

In the Union Army, they formed a strong, dependable military resource. Union officers soon became aware of the need for their impressive skills and readily used them.

A reenactor may elect to represent a free or enslaved person skilled as a craftsman, or artisan. In the role of skilled persons, reenactors need to learn how and by whom people of color were trained and whether or not they received wages for their labor.

Many were trained as apprentices under white people skilled in particular occupations. Skilled slaves were hired out to labor for others who paid their slave owners. Sometimes, the slaves were permitted to keep a fraction of their earnings. Eventually, some saved enough money to purchase their freedom from a willing master. Free Negroes usually worked in towns and were paid for their work.

Most textile production in the southern states was done by slaves. Females in bondage became expert spinners and weavers of cloth. Many developed expertise as seamstresses and in other needle crafts like knitting and crocheting.

Reenactors dressed appropriately as skilled laborers during the Civil War will enlighten audiences to the fact that all persons in bondage did not work on sugar plantations nor in cotton, tobacco, and corn fields. Both slaves and "free people of color" possessed specialized skills as craftsmen and artisans. Those skilled slaves who escaped to Union lines, although unknown by name, gave service to the Union during the war. These are important roles for people of color to interpret as reenactors. The bibliography at the end of the text lists titles which include information about the occupations of people of color.

In addition to printed biographies on specific characters, information is available from computer sources. Specific topics as "Blacks in the Civil War," "Civil War Heroines" or the names of persons as listed in this chapter, may be entered on sites like www.Google.com to obtain biographical information.

Civilian "People of Color"

Fig. 17. Reenactor Sarah Rone in 1860s fashions appropriate for a civilian role.

Reenactors who select a specific character's role should read one or more biographies about that person. It is essential that the reenactor be prepared to recite a brief summary of that person's life highlighting his or her service in the Civil War. Reenactors should view photographs of the character in order to see the hair styles of that period and to determine how that person dressed. No female makeup, modern watches, jewelry, modern eye glasses, or hair styles should be worn by anyone while wearing 1860s style clothing. Reenactors should be as authentic in appearance as possible. If the character portrayed had been a slave in his or her early life, like Frederick Douglass or Elizabeth Keckley, the reenactor may choose to portray that person either dressed as a slave or as a free person in his or her latter years.

At Civil War reenactments, whether one is dressed in the role of a specific character or whether one is interpreting the role of an unknown character by name, all reenactors serve an important part of the general population during the Civil War years.

A good feeling emerges as reenactors stroll around mingling with people. As speakers, they actively educate listeners about the role of black people in the Civil War. Only with all segments of the population represented, is the Civil War Reenactment scene complete.

For as much time as allowed and needed, every reenactor should have sufficient knowledge to enable him or her to talk about the life experiences of the character he or she is interpreting.

Brief biographies of Negro civilians and military men who served in the Civil War are included in this chapter on the pages that follow. Models dressed as reenactors in 1860s clothing are shown representing the various characters. Reenactors may select either of these characters to portray. Through further reading, others may be identified for historic interpretation.

1. Quarles, Benjamin. The Negro in the Civil War. Boston: Little, Brown & Co., 1968.

Harriet Tubman, Abolitionist, Scout, Spy, Guide and Nurse

During the beginning months of the Civil War, Governor John Andrew of Massachusetts invited Harriet Tubman to travel to Port Royal, South Carolina to serve as a scout, guide, nurse and spy for the Union soldiers stationed on the Sea Islands. When Harriet received the message that her services were needed, she willingly accepted the challenge to serve the Union cause and went to the Sea Islands on the coast of South Carolina.

When the Federals in Union gunboats reclaimed the islands, the planters abandoned their houses and slaves. Union officers established their headquarters there and moved into the mansions. Harriet Tubman occupied one of them.

Fig.18. Reenactor Ernestine Johnson as Harriet Tubman

After the secessionists (the white folks on the South Carolina sea coast islands) fled, their slaves became free. Young male slaves volunteered their service and became the 1st South Carolina Volunteers. Colonel Thomas Wentworth Higginson was assigned commander of this first regiment of black soldiers.

Before the war, Harriet had escaped from Dorchester County, Maryland to the free states, first arriving in Philadelphia in 1849. During the following years before the beginning of the Civil War, she had led hundreds of men, women and children to freedom including her aged parents, brothers and sisters. She lived for awhile in Canada after the 1850 Fugitive Slave Law was passed. This law made it unsafe for any slave fugitive to reside in a free state. Any citizen could apprehend the person, place him or her in jail, and notify the slave owner who would come to reclaim his human property. It did not matter how long the person had lived as free. So escaping slaves continued northward to Canada.

Harriet Tubman

Before the war, Harriet Tubman's courageous travels led her through secret passageways in towns and thick wooded areas to lead bands of escaped slaves to freedom. She became familiar with the terrain, a skill which enabled her to give very useful information to Union officers. Following familiar trails, she discovered Confederate positions and led raids into their strongholds. She learned the location of their storage places for food, supplies, weapons, and ammunition. "Her most valuable service to the Union was as a spy and scout....She headed a corps of local black men, most of them river pilots. Dressed as a freedwoman with a bandanna on her head, this short plain woman could travel anywhere in Rebel territory without arousing suspicion. When she and her scouts returned from their forays, she was able to pinpoint the location of cotton warehouses, ammunition depots and slaves who were waiting to be liberated. Noted as a guerrilla fighter, Colonel James Montgomery made numerous expeditions in the coastal areas of South Carolina, Georgia and Florida based on information from Harriet Tubman and her squad." (l, p.259)

As a nurse, she prepared concoctions for wounded and sick soldiers including Confederate prisoners in Union camps. She guided an expedition into Confederate territory under Colonel Montgomery down the Combahee River. They brought away hundreds of heads of livestock. Counted among the Confederate property taken were seven-hundred fifty-six contrabands.

Before returning to Auburn New York at the end of the war, Harriet was employed as matron of the Colored Hospital at Fortress Monroe.

In spite of her claims and despite letters from military and government officials, including a petition from Secretary of State William H. Seward to the United States Congress requesting recognition for her service, Harriet received no financial rewards from the government. For her services as nurse, scout, spy, and guide during all four years of the Civil War, she never received a pension from the government.

Harriet Tubman dictated accounts of her life story and Civil War experiences to Sarah Bradford. Bradford titled the book <u>Harriet Tubman, The Moses of Her people.</u> Harriet, aware of the needs of her aging parents, had the proceeds from book sales used to establish a home for the aged in Auburn. Harriet Tubman's life was completely devoted to being a servant helping people find freedom before and during the years of the war. She lived a long life and passed away March 10, 1913. The exact year of her birth is not known but was reported to be about the year 1820 in Dorchester County, Maryland.

Fig. 19. Harriet Tubman *Library of Congress #LCUSZ 62-7816*

For reenacting in the role of Harriet Tubman, Harriet Tubman, The Moses of Her people. by Sarah Bradford (Secaucus, NJ: Carol Publishing Group, 1997) should be read.

Well worth learning and repeating is this memorable quote of Harriet Tubman explaining her mission in life:

"Long 'go when de Lord tole me to go free my people, I said, "No Lord! I can't go--don't ask me." But he come anoder time. I saw him jes as plain, Den, I said again, "Lord, go away--get some better edicated person--get a person wid more cultur dan I have; go way Lord." But he cam back de third time, and speaks to me jess as he did to Moses, and he says, : "Harriet, I wants you," and I knew den I must do what he bid me. Now do you s'pose he wanted me to do dis jess for a day, or a week? No! de Lord who tole me take care of my people meant me to do it jess so long as I live and so I do what he told me to." (1.p.397, photograph p. 68.)

1. Sterling, Dorothy. We Are Your Sisters. Black Women in the Nineteenth Century. NY: W.W. Norton, 1984.

Fig. 20. Sisters Mary and Emily Edmondson
Library Of Congress USZ62-104364

Dresses, hairstyles and clothing appear appropriate for teens as reenactors.
These dresses have narrow white detachable collars and cuffs.

Teenagers may consider becoming interpreters of history. By wearing period clothing and reading extensively to become knowledgeable about important people, places, and events; young people can educate themselves and others. Opportunities for sharing historic facts exist at reenactments, as well as in schools, churches, parks, museums, libraries, and other places. They may be sponsored by religious, civic, and social organizations. Reenacting supports school social studies activities, especially "living history" projects.

Mary Elizabeth Bowser, Spy

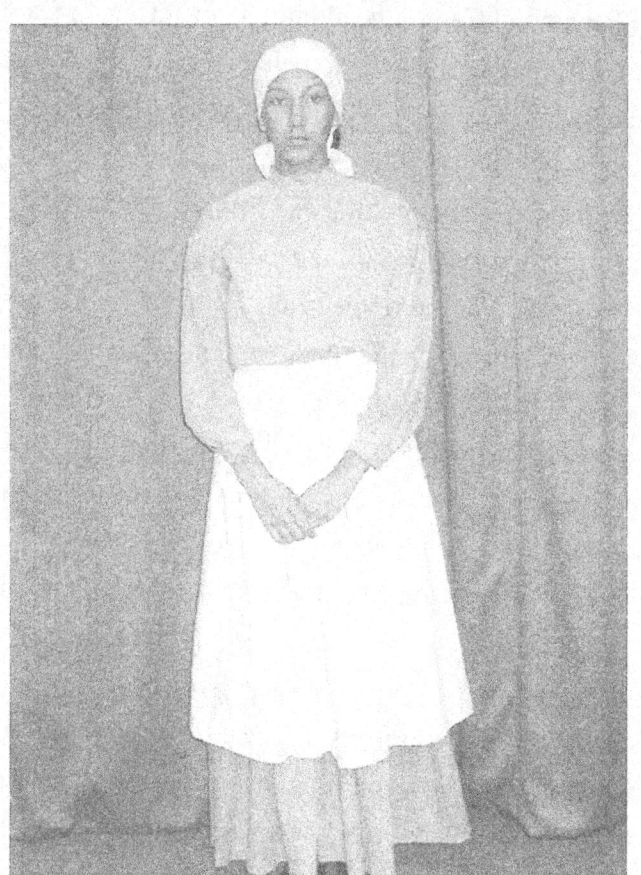

The story of Mary Elizabeth Bowser reads like one of mystery and intrigue. It began like those of many people of color in the South before the Civil War. Mary Elizabeth, born a slave, was purchased by the Van Lew family as a servant and playmate companion for the Van Lew's daughter, Elizabeth Louisa Van Lew. The girls grew up together and formed a close bond of friendship.

The Richmond, VA slave master, John Van Lew died in 1843. His widow and daughter Elizabeth purchased and freed his slaves. Elizabeth Louisa Van Lew attended school in Philadelphia. While there, she heard the story about the anguish of a slave mother whose baby was sold away from her. Elizabeth Louisa returned home an avid abolitionist determined to fight against slavery.

Fig. 21. Reenactor Virginia Smith as Mary Elizabeth Bowser

Elizabeth Louisia Van Lew recognized the intellect of Mary Elizabeth, her childhood slave companion. She paid the expenses for her to attend the Quaker School for Negroes in Philadelphia. As a free person, Mary Elizabeth moved to a Northern state to live. (Little is known about her life, either as a Van Lew slave or her life before she returned to Richmond or after the signing of the Emancipation Proclamation January 1, 1863.)

When the Civil War began, Elizabeth Louisa Van Lew at age 43, decided to serve the Union cause as a spy. Her goals were to defeat the South and to end slavery. Her code name was "Mr. Babcock." She asked Mary Elizabeth to return from the North and join her efforts to secure Confederate military secrets to pass on to Union officers. Van Lew enlisted the joint help of her mother, other family members, and servants in her spying efforts. Because of the way she dressed and conducted herself in her spying activities, Elizabeth Louisa became known as "Crazy Bet."

After returning to Richmond, Mary Elizabeth married Wilson Bowser. Even though she was free, intelligent, and well-educated; when Elizabeth Louisa Van Lew successfully arranged for Mary Elizabeth to work as a slave in the Richmond Capitol headquarters of Jefferson Davis, Mary Elizabeth Bowser accepted. She disguised herself as a slave and behaved as if she were illiterate. While Mary Elizabeth Bowser, disguised as an ignorant slave, served meals and took care of President Davis' children as their nurse, she listened to Confederate officers discuss military plans. She worked in the Davis White house from 1863 almost until the end of the war.

Robert W. Waitt reported "Her (Miss Van Lew's) colored girl Mary was the best as she was working right in Davis' home and (she) had a photographic mind. Everything she saw on the Rebel President's desk she could repeat word for word....She made a point of always coming out to my wagon when I made deliveries at the Davis' home to drop information (off on me)."(1, p.12) She saw official documents and memorized them. She passed what she learned discreetly to Elizabeth Van Lew who placed the messages in code and sent them to Union General Ulysses S. Grant. The secret code messages were sometimes placed in empty egg shells as one method of concealing their contents. Bowser risked her life passing through Confederate lines to deliver messages.

She also helped Elizabeth Van Lew to hide escaping Union prisoners. From them, they gathered information heard in discussions by Confederate prison guards. Bowser and Van Lew made visits to carry food and medicine to captured Union soldiers in Richmond warehouses and Libby Prison. Throughout the war, slaves served successfully as spies for the Union. This was true because as slaves, in the eyes of southerners, they were viewed as a common part of the landscape and not given conscious recognition of their presence.

Reenactors should read David D. Ryan's book in which he quotes from Elizabeth Louisa Van Lew's journal. A brief biography and photograph of Mary Elizabeth Bowser can be seen on the internet. Go to www.Google.com and type in the name Mary Elizabeth Bowser.

1. Ryan, David. D. A Yankee Spy in Richmond: The Civil War Diary of "Crazy Bet" Van Lew. Mechanicsburg: Stackpole Books, 1996.

Bibliography

Colman, Penny. Spies!: Women in the Civil War. White Hall: Shoe Tree Press, 1992.

Ryan, David. D. A Yankee Spy in Richmond: The Civil War Diary of "Crazy Bet" Van Lew.
    Mechanicsburg: Stackpole Books, 1996.

Charlotte Forten, Teacher

Fig. 22. Reenactor Merceda Nicholson as Charlotte Forten

Charlotte Forten, a free person of color, was born in August, 1837 in Philadelphia into a very wealthy free family. Her mother died when she was age three and her father when she was seven. She was reared by her grandparents. Charlotte was taught by her family at home and later sent to Salem, Massachusetts to live with relatives and attend Salem Normal School to be trained as a teacher. Her grand father, James Forten, was born in 1866. He attended a Quaker school and served in the Revolutionary War. He became a prisoner during the war and stayed for seven months in a British ship anchored near the American shore. James was released after he was exchanged for a British prisoner. Forten later worked for ship builder Robert Bridges who sold the business to him. The business thrived and James became very wealthy.

Charlotte began to keep a journal at age fourteen. From her journal entries, readers learn about her and the lives of people of color during the Civil War. Charlotte wrote poetry. Some of her poems were published in the *Liberator,* an abolitionist newspaper published by William Lloyd Garrison. Her grandfather made contributions for the publication of that paper. Charlotte's aunt and uncle were Harriet and Robert Purvis. Their home in the countryside of Philadelphia was used as a station on the Underground Railroad. The Forten family members were all staunch active abolitionists.

Charlotte met the poet, John Greenleaf Whittier. He encouraged her to travel to the Sea Islands off the coast of South Carolina to teach the children of contrabands (children of escaped slaves) and the slave children left on the island after the slave owners made a hasty departure when Federals recaptured the islands.

Charlotte Forten

In 1862 when Charlotte was 24 years old, she boarded a ship for St. Helena Island, South Carolina. The country was engaged in the Civil War which had begun with the bombardment at Fort Sumter near Charleston.

When the ship docked, she was shocked to see the barefooted, ragged, poor condition of former slaves. At the beginning of the conflict, Union soldiers took over the chain of islands along the Georgia, Florida, and South Carolina coasts on the day of the "Big Gun Shoot, November 7, 1862." The "Secession Buckra," (so called by the Sea Island slaves) or white plantation owners, abandoned their elaborate plantation houses and thereby set their slaves free.

The first regiment of black Union soldiers was organized on the islands. Charlotte met Colonel Thomas Wentworth Higginson, commander of the South Carolina First Colored Troops on the day when the Emancipation Proclamation was first read at Camp Saxon, South Carolina.

She wrote in her journal about that memorable day when she attended the first reading of the proclamation and was a part of the celebration on January 1, 1863. As she heard the reading of Lincoln's great instrument of freedom, she witnessed tears that swelled in the eyes of Colonel Thomas Wentworth Higginson as he spoke and joined the rejoicing of former slaves and soldiers present. A dress parade of the Union troops followed the program.

Charlotte was on a nearby island when the Battle at Fort Wagner was fought on Morris Island July 18, 1863. It was the battle in which the Massachusetts 54th Infantry suffered severe casualties and their commander, Colonel Robert Shaw, lost his life as he led his troops into the battle. In her diary, Charlotte recalled that she was greatly impressed when she met the young commander of the 54th, Colonel Shaw. He was only 25 years old, well respected, and loved by all of the men under his command.

On Tuesday, July 21, three days after the battle, Charlotte asked Ellen Murray to teach her classes. She had heard that wounded soldiers of the Fifty-fourth had been brought from Morris Island to Port Royal and that the hospital at Beaufort needed nurses. She went to Port Royal and Beaufort, South Carolina to offer her services to the wounded. There she mended uniforms, gave out medicines and helped change bandages.

In her diary, Charlotte wrote, "It was with a full heart that I sewed up bullet holes and bayonet cuts. Sometimes I found a jacket that told a sad tale--so torn to pieces that it was far past mending."(1, pp.90-91)

Charlotte Forten is remembered as a free black woman who served as a teacher and one who aided wounded soldiers following the battle at Fort Wagner during the Civil War on the Sea Islands in South Carolina. Abolitionists from the North sent books and other materials for the children who were taught in a red brick church until a school house could be built.

Charlotte Forten

Teen and Pre-teen 1860s Style Dresses
Fig. 23. A child may select to wear an 1860s style dress to portray Charlotte Forten, who was born free and wealthy. (See Heidi Marsh's What Children Wore (Or Wished They Could) In The Era Of The Hoop.)

Reenactors may select Charlotte Forten or members of the Forten family as characters for living history interpretation at Civil War reenactments. She was from a wealthy family, so her clothing would have been in the latest and most affordable 1860s styles as a free person of color. Photographs of James and Robert Purvis, Charlotte Forten and other teachers with their contraband students are in Peter Burchard's biography of Charlotte Forten.

1. Burchard, Peter. Charlotte Forten, A Black Teacher in the Civil War. NY: Crown Publishers, 1995.

Mary Kelsey Peake, Teacher

Mary Kelsey Peake was born in Norfolk, VA in 1823. "She was one of the first African-American teachers in the South. Peake created a school for the 'contrabands of war' during the Civil War."

The above fact was discovered on the internet.

When Loretta Dabbs, a civilian Civil War reenactor, sought the name of a character to portray as a reenactor, she did what others are encouraged to do: search the internet.

Information about how "people of color" served in the Civil War can be as close as the keyboard on home computers. Once the name is discovered, then research should follow to learn more about the character in libraries and other research centers.

Fig. 24. Reenactor Loretta Dabbs as Mary Kelsey Peake

By the time of the Civil War, Mary Kelsey Peake was a free black, so a reenactor would dress in appropriate 1860s style clothing as worn by Loretta Dabbs.

In order to properly represent Mary Kelsey Peake, Loretta Dabbs acquired knowledge about her life to explain the same to visitors at reenactments.

Mary Kelsey Peake, became the wife of Thomas Peake, a free man, in 1851. Mary's husband Thomas served as a spy for the Union Army during the war. After Mary became a member of the First Baptist Church in Richmond, she founded a benevolent society and began to educate the children who attended the church. During the 1850s, she secretly taught both slave and free children. In the first year of the Civil War, she opened a model school for contrabands. The school was sponsored by the American Missionary Society. Her teaching methods were very much admired by others.

Elizabeth Keckley, Modiste to Mary Todd Lincoln

Fig. 25. Reenactor Yvette Birdsong as Elizabeth Keckley

Incidents in the Life of Elizabeth Keckley are told in her autobiography titled Behind the Scenes, or Thirty Years a Slave and Four Years in the White House. Elizabeth, the daughter of a slave mother, was born in 1820 in Virginia. However, from the circumstances of her appearance, Elizabeth's father was believed to have been her mother's slave master. He purchased Elizabeth's stepfather, her mother's husband, from another plantation with the promise that he would be retained so that Elizabeth's mother and father could live together. His promise was not kept. Instead, her stepfather was sold and sent out west permanently. For years, heart-touching correspondence passed between the family, but sadly, they were never reunited.

Elizabeth's real troubles began when she reached age 18 and was sent to North Carolina to live with a white man. With him, she bore an only son. She reported that her "troubles" ended in North Carolina when the daughter of her mother's slave master married a Mr. Garland. He was not a prosperous man, so envisioning a better life for his wife and family, he left Virginia departing for St. Louis, Missouri. He sent for Elizabeth, her son and her mother. In St. Louis, he fared no better as evidenced by his inability to even pay postage on a letter addressed to him at the post office. During those days, postage was paid by the recipients of letters.

Mr. Garland planned to hire out her mother to bring in money for the support of his family. Elizabeth staunchly opposed this plan. She expressed her objection and offered to support the

Garland family with income from her sewing skills. Elizabeth took care of seventeen people using her skills in sewing for a number of years. After two years, she asked for her freedom, but it was denied. After a second request for her freedom, Garland offered her a quarter to catch the ferry. He told her that once she crossed the river, she would have her freedom in a free state.

Elizabeth refused. She wanted to be manumitted by law. A slave within the borders of a free state without freedom papers was never safe. Under those conditions, anyone could claim her as his slave property. Elizabeth approached Mr. Garland relentlessly pleading to purchase freedom for herself and her son. Finally, he changed his mind and told her the purchase price for her freedom was $1200. She resolved to raise the money. With determination, she continued to sew for the leading ladies in Missouri, but her efforts to sew and save part of her earnings were not successful. In the meantime, Mr. Gardener died. A planter from Mississippi came to settle the estate. He agreed that she should be free and agreed to receive the purchase price. The funds were raised with the aid of her patrons, several most benevolent women. After Elizabeth purchased freedom for herself and her son, she decided to leave St. Louis. Elizabeth separated from her husband because she was displeased with his ways. Her mother traveled back to Virginia as a slave with Mrs. Garland.

Elizabeth and her son traveled to Washington, D.C. in 1860. There she boarded with a black Walker couple. Elizabeth opened a shop and started a successful dressmaking business. She later hired twenty women. She repaid the women who had so graciously aided her. Elizabeth's clients were the wives of the Congressmen.

Not long after her arrival in Washington, she began sewing for the wife of Jefferson Davis. One day while Elizabeth was adjusting a dress on Mrs. Davis in her home, Mrs. Davis, invited Elizabeth to travel to the South with her. In response, Elizabeth asked, "When do you go south?"

Mrs. Davis responded, "Oh, I cannot tell just now, but it will be soon." Then she added, "You know there is going to be war, Lizzie?"

...."Who will go to war?" Elizabeth asked.

Mrs. Davis replied, "The North and South."

...."And which do you think will whip?" asked Elizabeth.

Mrs. Davis' answer, "The South, of course."

Mrs. Davis ended this discussion of an upcoming war with the prediction, "As soon as we go south and secede from the other states, we will raise an army and march on Washington, and then I shall live in the White House."(1,pp.70-72)

Of course, history proved Mrs. Davis' prediction an error. Elizabeth's faithful service had engendered Mrs. Davis' confidence. Elizabeth gave the matter thought but considered it in her best interest not to accept her offer. When it became known that Mrs. Mary Todd Lincoln, wife of President Abraham Lincoln, was in need of a seamstress, Elizabeth's name was given to Mrs. Lincoln by one of her patrons, a Mrs. McClean. "Lizabeth," as she was called by Mrs. Lincoln, became her regular modiste (personal seamstress). President Lincoln addressed her as "Madam Elizabeth." To others, she was known as "Lizzie."

Although Elizabeth Keckley did not reside in the White House, she spent many hours there with Mrs. Lincoln and became her close friend and confidante. During Elizabeth's first year of employment, she made more than a dozen dresses for Mrs. Lincoln.

When the Civil War began, Elizabeth observed changing moods in the White House as stirring news of battles reached the President's ears. Amidst it all came the sad hours of uncontrollable grief of Mrs. Lincoln following the death of Willie Lincoln. Elizabeth shared the family's grief and was very understanding as she had lost her son in a Civil War battle in Missouri. Her son had enrolled at Wilberforce University and had withdrawn when the Civil War began to enlist in a white unit.

As the war progressed, together Elizabeth and Mrs. Lincoln visited the wounded and dying soldiers in a hospital near Washington. Since Mrs. Lincoln had come from the South, folks wondered about and questioned her loyalty in the conflict. She was a supporter of the Union.

Elizabeth Keckley rendered remarkable service to the former slaves during the Civil War. She was joined by Harriet Jacobs, who titled her autobiography Incidents in the Life of a Slave Girl. (NY: Penquin Putnam, Inc., 2000, first published in Boston, 1861). When Harriet first arrived in the Capitol city after promoting her book in Pennsylvania, 400 homeless fugitive slaves were there. A year later, there were about ten thousand and by the end of the war, about forty thousand in need of every subsistence for life. Harriet remained in the District to assist the refugees.

She tended the sick, solicited and distributed clothing and helped them to find jobs. In an 1862 letter to William Lloyd Garrison, Harriet requested help from its readers. She described the plight of the contrabands when she wrote:

> "Some of them have been so degraded by slavery that they do not know
> the usages of civilized life; they know little else than the handle of the hoe,
> the plow, the cotton pod and the overseer's lash. Have patience with
> them. You have helped to make them what they are; teach them civilization.
> You owe it to them and you will find them as apt to learn as any other people
> that come to you stupid from oppression." (2,pp.246-247)

Elizabeth Keckley

In 1862, as those former slaves, or contrabands, poured into the Capitol city of Washington, Elizabeth Keckley saw their urgent need for food, clothing, and shelter. They had their freedom but little else. Elizabeth raised funds to help them. Those poor people had left their plantations, joined the Yankee lines, and ended up in Washington, D.C. Elizabeth formed a Contraband Relief Association. She shared in the founding of a Home for Destitute Women and Children and raised money at churches and solicited funds from individuals. Frederick Douglass gave $200. Monetary contributions and boxes of clothing and other goods were sent from churches. President and Mrs. Lincoln made frequent contributions. Funds were received from as far away as Edinburgh, Scotland, Bristol, England, and locally from Boston and abolitionist societies in the northern states.

Keckley's book, <u>Behind the Scenes,</u> gives readers a glance into Lincoln's White House during the final years of the Civil War and its crisis aftermath, the assassination of President Lincoln. Mrs. Lincoln sent for Elizabeth to be continually at her side as a source of comfort during the saddest episode of her life and that of the country. Elizabeth was the only companion of Mrs. Lincoln as her husband's body was borne 1700 miles to its final resting place. Elizabeth was more than a simple servant possessed with superb sewing skills; she was Mrs. Lincoln's trusted and beloved friend.

Reenactors who select the role of Elizabeth Keckley or Harriet Jacobs should read their books. Clothing can be representative of the women as slaves or as free people. Both Elizabeth Keckley and Harriet Jacobs rendered commendable service to fugitive slaves (contrabands) during the Civil War.

Elizabeth is quoted as having said, "I dressed Mrs. Lincoln for every levee. I made every stitch of clothing that she wore. I dressed her hair. I put on her skirts and dresses. I fixed her bouquets, saw that her gloves were all right, and remained with her each evening until Mr. Lincoln came for her. My hands were the last to touch her before she took the arm of Mr. Lincoln and went forth to meet the ladies and gentlemen on those great occasions." Elizabeth Keckley's photograph appears in her book.

1. Keckley, Elizabeth. <u>Behind the Scenes, or Thirty Years a Slave and Four Years in the White House.</u> NY: Oxford Univ. Pr. 1988.

2. Sterling, Dorothy. <u>We Are Your Sisters, Black Women in the Nineteenth Century.</u> NY: W.W. Norton, 1984.

Susie King Taylor, Nurse

Fig. 26. Reenactor Azza Thames as Susie King Taylor

Susie King Taylor, like Harriet Tubman, Charlotte Forten, and Clara Barton, was a woman who rendered nursing service to wounded soldiers during the Civil War on the Sea Islands on the South Carolina coast. No one can question the importance of that service. Clara Barton was a white nurse who tended to black soldiers after the Battle of Fort Wagner. Barton, the founder of the American Red Cross, wrote: "I can see again the scarlet flow of blood as it rolled over the black limbs beneath my hands..."(1,pp.16,228)

Within published accounts of their lives spent on the islands, those women met each other. Susie accompanied Clara Barton as she made rounds in the hospital during Clara Barton's eight months on the Sea Islands. (2, p.72)

Susie, like Charlotte Forten, was also present at Camp Saxon on January 1, 1863 for the first reading of the Emancipation Proclamation. She described it as a "glorious day for all and we enjoyed every minute of it and as a fitting close and the crowning event of this occasion, we had a grand barbecue...The soldiers had a good time. They sang or shouted 'Hurrah!' all through the camp and seemed overflowing with fun and frolic until taps were sounded, when many no doubt, dreamt of this memorable day."(2, p.49, 50)

Susie King Taylor was born August 6, 1848 on an island off the coast of Savannah, Georgia. Susie knew what many born into slavery never knew, and that was facts about her unusual genealogy. Her maternal great-great-grandmother, born in Virginia, was half Indian. She had seven children and five of her sons served in the Revolutionary War. Susie's great-great grandmother's daughter Susanna had twenty-four children and twenty-three were girls. She died at age 100, while Susie's great-great grandmother had lived to be 120.

Susie King Taylor

Although Susie's mother was a slave, her maternal grandmother was a "free person of color." She lived in Savannah. As a free person, she had to have a white guardian. Her mother's slave master, Mr. Grest, assumed that role. Susie's mother was married to Raymond Baker. They were the parents of nine children. Three died in infancy. Susie was the oldest of her surviving siblings.

When Susie was a child of seven, her mother's slave master allowed her to live with her grandmother, Dolly Reed, in Savannah. Her grandmother knew Mrs. Woodhouse, a free black who secretly taught a small group of children in her kitchen. Susie and the other pupils walked through the streets to and from this makeshift schoolroom in very small groups with their books hidden.

Black children, according to law, were forbidden to learn how to read and write. They were whipped if caught with books. However, Susie learned from Mrs. Woodhouse and three white childhood friends to whom she promised not to divulge their secret. She wrote passes for many slaves in order for them to be out after the evening's curfew. Susie's meager education enabled her to teach others.

When the Civil War began, Susie was thirteen years old. She joined her uncle and his family when they escaped from Savannah on board a Union gunboat on the Georgia coast. When the men on the boat learned that Susie could read and write, she began to teach them during their off-duty hours. Susie's father served on a gun boat during the war.

They were taken to one of the Sea Islands along the coast of South Carolina. The finest cotton grew on those islands. The slaves, isolated from the mainland, labored in the cotton fields. When the planters abandoned the islands fleeing from the advancing Federals in gun boats, the slaves became free. Attention was devoted to beginning schools for the former slave children. Susie, like Charlotte Forten, began teaching the children. She was a teenage teacher of forty children during the day and a teacher of adult former slaves at night. When an order was received to evacuate the island, Susie was enrolled as a laundress with the regiment under Colonel Thomas Wentworth Higginson, the 1st South Carolina Volunteers. They were all former slaves.

Susie related her Civil War service in great detail in her memoirs initially published in 1902 in Boston, titled <u>Reminiscences of My Life in Camp with the 33rd U. S. Colored Troops, Late 1st South Carolina Volunteers.</u> She actually joined the 1st South Carolina Volunteers, the first regiment of blacks in the Civil War. (The regiment was renamed the 33rd U. S. Colored Troops.)

Susie King Taylor

While in camp, Susie busied herself as a laundress, nurse, and cook. She followed the soldiers from camp to camp and even traveled as far as Florida. In her "Reminiscences," she described her living-in-tent experiences among the soldiers. After one battle she wrote, "When the wounded arrived or began to arrive...My work now began. I gave my assistance to try to alleviate their sufferings. I asked the doctor at the hospital what I could get for them to eat. They wanted soup, but that I could not get; but I had a few cans of condensed milk and some turtle eggs, so I thought I would try to make some custard...cooking with turtle eggs was something new to me...I made a venture and the result was a very delicious custard."(2,p.90)

Susie gave service for the comfort of those men. She stated, "I was enrolled as company laundress, but I did very little of it because I was always busy doing other things through camp and employed all the time doing something for the officers and comrades."(2,p.91)

She expressed pride in her ability to take apart the guns, clean and reassemble them. She boasted of her ability to shoot straight. She accompanied the regiments during the capture of Charleston after it was set on fire by the rebels. In March 1863, Susie was with the 1st South Carolina Regiment when they embarked in Jacksonville, Florida and faced pickets and skirmishes with General Finegan's Confederate troops.

Susie married Sergeant Edward King, a literate black of the 1st South Carolina Volunteers, in 1862 but the marriage was short-lived. He was skilled as a carpenter. Edward died in 1866 before the birth of their first child. After the war, Susie began a private school in Savannah and later, another school in Liberty County, Georgia. Both schools were forced to close when a free school opened in each place. She moved to Boston, entered domestic service, and remarried.

For reenacting, a living history portrayal of Susie King Taylor as a nurse during the Civil War, is an excellent choice. Her book titled, Reminiscences of My Life, A Black Woman's Civil War Memoirs, should be read by the reenactor. Taylor gives readers an understanding of the valuable service rendered by former slave women in Union camps during the Civil War. Her account of service within the 1st South Carolina Volunteers is unparalleled in giving a description of troop movements and day-to-day encounters with rebels. A seamstress should be able to make an outfit like the one she is wearing in her book or the reenactor may dress as a free person since Susie King Taylor was a free person during the Civil War.

1. Quarles, Benjamin. Negroes in the Civil War. Boston, 1955.

2. Taylor, Susie King. Reminiscences of my Life, A Black Woman's Civil War Memoirs. NY: Markus Wiener Publishing, 1988.

Fig. 27. Unidentified Woman in 1860s Style Dress

This woman has the look appropriate for an older woman desirous of being economic, yet fashionable in the 1860s. The two-piece dress is made from a solid shade of soft fabric with a small white detachable ribbon neck band, and a pin to clasp it. The sleeves are trimmed with the same fabric. The bodice touches the natural waistline. The buttoned-front waist appears to be tucked into the skirt band. Dropped shoulder seams attach long sleeves from the curve of the shoulders. Sleeves are wide at the elbow. Although not seen, the dress length probably reaches to three or four inches from the floor. The wide soft-pleated skirt covers a hoop. The hair is pulled back above the ears. She does not appear to be wearing jewelry.

Sojourner Truth, Abolitionist/Supporter

Fig. 28. Sojourner Truth and Abraham Lincoln
Library of Congress USZ62-16225

Sojourner Truth, whose birth name was Isabella Baumfree, like Harriet Tubman, is an excellent character for portrayals at Civil War reenactments. She was an active abolitionist after she walked away from her slave master to free herself in New York a year before a law was passed in 1827 abolishing slavery in New York. At the beginning of the Civil War, she helped recruit black men to help in the war effort and during the war, she carried food to black regiments. She raised funds at her lectures to purchase food and gifts for the servicemen. The people of Detroit prepared a Thanksgiving dinner for the 102nd U.S. Colored Infantry stationed at Camp Ward near Detroit, Michigan. Sojourner delivered the food to the men.

Sojourner is remembered most for her service as an abolitionist and a spokesperson for the rights of women. However, she avidly supported the recruitment of blacks for the Union forces.

Recruiters

"After the War Department authorized regiments of free blacks, the last lingering doubts about the goals of the war disappeared. Black women quickly undertook the traditional work of women in wartime--preparing food and clothing for the soldiers; sewing regimental flags and writing letters to the front. Black troops were in demand. Prominent men, including *Frederick Douglass, William Wells Brown* and *Charles L. Remond* became recruiting agents. Paid by the states, they traveled as far as Canada and to Union-held territory in the South to obtain black volunteers. They were aided by women like *Josephine Ruffin, and Harriet Jacobs,* who wrote from

Fig. 29. Reenactor Matherlyn Smith as Sojourner Truth

Alexandria, 'I hope to obtain some recruits for the Massachusetts Cavalry, not for money, but because I want to do all I can to strengthen the hands of those who are battling for freedom.' *Mary Ann Shadd Cary* who had been supporting her two children by teaching school became the only woman officially commissioned as a recruiting agent. She was brought to the work by her friend Martin R. Delany...."(1, pp.256-257) Delany of the 104th USCT, who was the first black staff officer in the history of the United States military. (2,p.118)

Reenactors may read Sojourner Truth's biography to learn about her life experiences and role in the Civil War. Each of the persons whose names are printed in italics in the second paragraph (See Recruiters) are excellent choices for reenactment roles. Information about each one is accessible on the internet. Books about them are available in libraries.

1. Sterling, Dorothy. <u>We Are Your Sisters. Black Women in the Nineteenth Century.</u> NY: W.W. Norton, 1984. (See Sojourner Truth's photograph, p.152)

See also Krass, Peter. <u>Sojourner Truth. Antislavery Activist.</u> NY: Chelsea House, 1988.

2. Tucker, Phillip Thomas. <u>Civil War Chronicles From Auction Block to Glory. The African American Experience</u>. NY: Friedman Publishing Group, 1998.

Frederick Douglass, Recruiter

The most notable of the recruiters was Frederick Douglass. He was born in 1817, a slave of Hugh Auld. Douglass escaped in September, 1838 by disguising himself in the uniform of a sailor. Frederick became one of many "fpc" living in New York and other free states.

Fig. 30. Frederick Douglass
Library of Congress LC-USZ62-7825

His disguise as a sailor with borrowed seaman's papers determined the route of Douglass' escape. It was chosen because he had been sent by his master to work for his brother in a Baltimore shipyard as a caulker.

Once a free man, Douglass became an avid abolitionist speaking about his slave experiences and serving as a conductor on the Underground Railroad assisting other fugitives. His home became a station on the Underground Railroad.

When Douglas heard the 1860 inaugural address of President Abraham Lincoln, he was disappointed when Lincoln said he would not interfere with slavery in the South. Although Lincoln personally opposed slavery and had never owned slaves, he wanted to preserve the Union. (For Lincoln's views about slavery, see Appendix B Lincoln's letter to a friend, Joshua F. Speed, dated August 25, 1855.)

After the Confederates attacked Fort Sumter on April 12, 1861, Lincoln called for troops but not for black people to serve. Douglass was encouraged by the president's actions against slavery when he signed a bill in 1862 that outlawed slavery in Washington, D.C. and in September, 1862 when he stated that "If the Confederates did not cease fighting by January 1, 1863, he would issue a proclamation to free all of the slaves in the states in rebellion against the Union." The Emancipation Proclamation was signed and became law January 1, 1863. After that date, black men could be mustered into the Union Army.

Douglass had continually urged President Lincoln to arm black men to fight. Lincoln's Emancipation Proclamation had opened the way. However, earlier in Louisiana, Kansas and South Carolina, some black units had been organized, but dismissed.

Douglass became a recruiting agent for John A. Andrew, Governor of Massachusetts, who was authorized to raise black units. Douglass' first recruits were his two sons Charles and Lewis Douglass. It was difficult to recruit blacks for several reasons: unequal pay with white soldiers; inability to become commissioned officers; and fear of being cast into slavery if captured by the Confederates or killed rather than being perceived and treated as prisoners of war.

Lincoln assured Douglass that black soldiers would eventually receive equal pay. Even with the knowledge that they would not receive equal pay, thousands of black men volunteered for the Union Army. The majority of them were former slaves.

"Shortly after the Confederate surrender, Major Martin Delany, one of the highest ranking black officers in the war, announced to a black audience, 'Do you know that if it was not for the black men, this war never would have been brought to a close with success to the Union and the liberty of your race if it had not been for the Negro?'

"These words sound bold, perhaps even overblown. But his statement differed little from Abraham Lincoln's own assessment." As the following quote implies, Lincoln foresaw emancipation and black enlistment as the policy that would eventually win the war. 'I believe it is a resource which if vigorously applied right now, will soon close out the contest,' he predicted to Grant.(1.p.53) Even President Lincoln had predicted in mid-1863 that "emancipation and black enlistment would eventually win the war." Lincoln's quote is significantly noteworthy for the credit it gives to black men who fought and died for the freedom of people in bondage and the Union cause.

Frederick Douglass, a "free person of color," was an outstanding orator, a great abolitionist, and an effective recruiter of black men to serve in the Civil War.

Reenactors may reenact the role of Frederick Douglass dressed appropriately as a slave or Douglass as a free man. Many photographs of him appear in countless Civil War publications and other books including the Ebony Classics Edition of Frederick Douglass' biography titled, <u>My Bondage and My Freedom.</u> (Chicago: Johnson Publishing Co., 1970).

1. Glatthaar, Joseph. <u>The Civil War's Black Soldiers, Civil War Series.</u> Eastern National Park and Monument Association, 1996.

Henry McNeal Turner, Military Chaplain

Fig. 31. Rev. Michael A. Frazier as Chaplain Henry McNeal Turner

The honorable distinction of being the first black man appointed by President Abraham Lincoln as a regular army chaplain during the Civil War belongs to Rev. Henry McNeal Turner. He was attached to the 1st Regiment, United States Colored Troops of South Carolina in 1863. He remained in that position until President Andrew Johnson appointed him the first Chaplain of the regular United States Army and assigned him to the Georgia office of the Freedmen's Bureau after the war. There were 158 black regiments in the Union Army. Twelve of the regiments had black chaplains. When the Civil War began, Turner lobbied for the enlistment of black troops. As a friend of Edwin Stanton, he helped to sway President Lincoln to enlist them.

Turner, the son of free parents, was born near Abbeville County, South Carolina on February 1, 1834. Turner was a very young boy when his father died. He was apprenticed to a blacksmith. Turner's education began at age 15 during his employment in a lawyer's office. The men in the office recognized his ability and taught him the rudiments of reading, writing, and arithmetic. He joined the Methodist Episcopal Church and in 1853 was licensed as a preacher. In 1872, he received an LL.D. degree from the University of Pennsylvania. Chaplain Turner became chancellor of Morris Brown College in Atlanta, GA.

Reenacting in the role of Henry McNeal Turner, a free person of color, would require dressing as a male *fpc* before the Civil War or in the uniform of a soldier during the Civil War. Information on the internet tells about Turner's family life and service. Go to www.Google.com. Reenactors may view illustrations of male 1860s style suits in this text for examples of the way Turner may have attired himself as a civilian minister. (See page 78.)

Some information about Henry McNeal Turner is in Troubling Biblical Waters: Race, Class and Family, Vol. 3 by Cain Hope Felder. (Maryknoll, NY: Orbis Books, 1989.)

A FREE FAMILY OF COLOR

Fig. 32. AN 1860s FAMILY OF ST. JOSEPH, MISSOURI
Courtesy, Collection of Deborah Fontana Cooney

Persons interested in portraying the services of free black people during the Civil War may consider the clothing styles of this family. The husband's wool suit is trimmed with braid and he wears a narrow bow tie and vest. His wife's dress is a small floral print with a fitted waist and satin ribbon trimming on the waist and arm sleeves. The collar is white. The dress may be made from light wool or cotton fabric and worn over a hoop. The boys are dressed in dark colored Zouave jackets with tab closures. They are wearing white long sleeve shirts and long pants which match their jackets. The pants are pleated at the waist and buttoned over the shirts.

Robert Smalls, Seaman

Although black enlistment in the Union Army at the beginning of the Civil War met great resistance, the Federal Navy welcomed blacks. It had never barred free Negroes. As early as September 1861, a policy to accept former slaves was adopted. Blacks in the navy were treated well and they proved to be most useful. One quarter of the navy men in the Union fleet were blacks, or 29,511 out of 118.044.(1, p.230) Blacks filled every rank on Union vessels including service as pilots. Navigating the waterways required experience which many fugitive slaves had acquired before the war.

Fig. 33. Reenactor Kenneth O. Mitchell as Robert Smalls
Library of Congress 826-825

A most outstanding hero of the Union Navy was Robert Smalls, an escaped slave. Smalls was owned by Robert and Lydia Smalls of Beaufort, South Carolina.

His birth was recorded as April 5, 1839. He grew up in Charleston. When a young man, he was taken aboard a Confederate transport steamer, the Planter. He had had experience piloting boats and was familiar with the currents and channels in Charleston Harbor. Smalls, like all others in bondage, desired his freedom. His opportunity came on the morning of May 13, 1862. While the white officers were asleep in Charleston, Smalls hastened from the ship and brought his family aboard. With his hands at the ship's helm, he raced out to sea beyond the range of Confederate guns. With the white flag of truce hoisted, Smalls piloted the Confederate transport ship smack into the welcomed nest of the Union fleet. This was a courageous and daring feat, which he described as a "contribution of black Americans to the cause of freedom." The Confederate ship was seized as contraband. Smalls and his crew of twelve were recognized as heroes and later rewarded for their courageous act by President Lincoln.

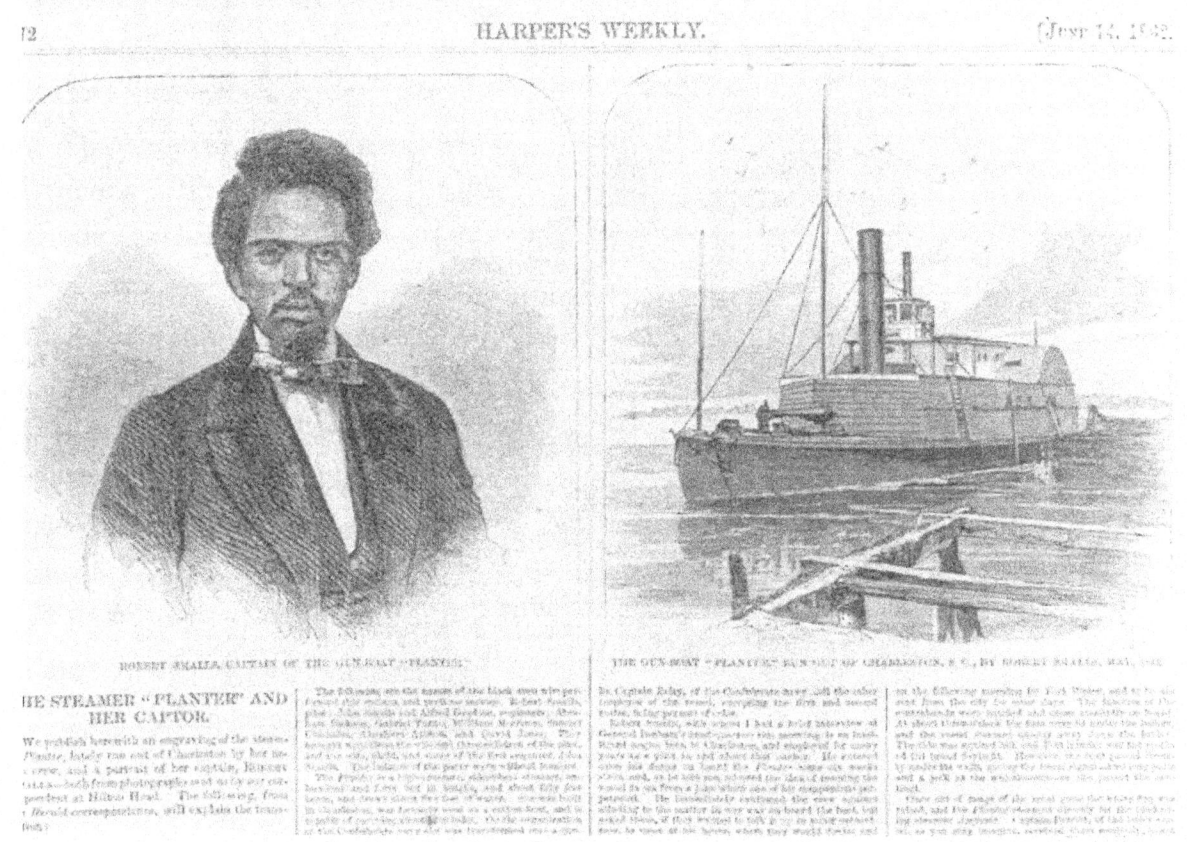

Fig. 34. Robert Smalls and the Confederate Ship, Planter
Library of Congress USZ62-11798

Reenactors in the role of Robert Smalls could dress as a male slave or search for a photograph of Civil War Union Naval Uniforms. A naval uniform could be made if the uniforms are not available through sutlers. Research on the internet may reveal sources.

1. Quarles, Benjamin. <u>The Negro in the Civil War.</u> Boston: Little, Brown & Co., 1968.

Mrs. Eileen Herr, a Civil War seamstress, makes garments for both military and civilian male reenactors. (See the sutler ads at the end of the text.)

Bibliography

Suggested titles of interest to reenactors. These books contain Civil War experiences of the persons whose biographies are included in Chapter 3.

Bradford, Sarah. <u>Harriet Tubman, the Moses of Her People.</u> Secaucus, NJ: Carol Publishing Group, 1997.
This book includes Tubman's life experiences and role in the Civil War.

<u>Burchard, Peter. Charlotte Forten, A Black Teacher in the Civil War.</u> NY: Crown Publishers, <u>1995.</u>
Charlotte, a free black born in Philadelphia to abolitionists, was educated as a teacher. She went to St. Helena Island, SC during the Civil War to teach the children of former slaves. A very interesting description of the Battle at Fort Wagner is included in the text.

Douglass, Frederick. <u>Life and Times of Frederick Douglass, His Early Life as a Slave, His Escape from Bondage and His Complete History.</u> NY: Macmillan Publishing Co., Inc., 1962.

Higginson, Thomas Wentworth. <u>Army Life in a Black Regiment.</u> N.Y.: Norton, 1984.
Colonel Higginson's account of his experiences as the commander of the first American regular army regiment of freed slaves. This book is a "must read" for every Civil War reenactor. "In the Mid-1860s it was widely understood that black soldiers in great numbers contributed mightily to the victory of the Union side in the Civil War." Quoted from the book's preface.

Jacobs, Harriet. <u>Incidents in the Life of a Slave Girl, Written by Herself, Linda Brent.</u> Boston: 1861. Reprint, Penguin Putnam, Inc., 2000.
This is an account of the author's life story as a slave.

Keckley, Elizabeth. <u>Behind the Scenes, or Thirty Years a Slave and Four Years in the White House.</u> NY: Oxford Univ. Pr. 1988.
The book includes the author's life experiences and role in the Civil War.

Krass, Peter. <u>Sojourner Truth, Antislavery Activist.</u> NY: Chelsea House, 1988.
Krass describes the life experiences of Sojourner Truth and her role in the Civil War.

<u>Lincoln His Words and His World.</u> Polley, Robert L., Editor and staff of *Country Beautiful*, Waukesha, Wisconsin. MCMLXV.

McCurdy, Michael. <u>Escape from Slavery, The Boyhood of Frederick Douglass in His Own Words.</u>* N.Y. Knopf, 1994.
A biography excerpted from Douglass' autobiography.

Quarles, Benjamin. <u>The Negro in the Civil War.</u> Boston: Little, Brown & Co., 1968.
A definitive study of Negroes in the Civil War: their service in the Union army, navy, and the vital role of contrabands as informants, scouts, spies and laborers.

Sterling, Dorothy. <u>We Are Your Sisters, Black Women in the Nineteenth Century.</u> NY: W.W. Norton, 1984.
A researched volume on the lives of American black women, before, during and after the Civil War.

Taylor, Susie King. <u>Reminiscences of My Life, A Black Woman's Civil War Memoirs.</u> NY: Markus Wiener Publishing, 1988.
The book includes the author's experiences and service in the Civil War.

Fig. 35. Slave Woman in Apron
Courtesy, New Hampshire Historical Society, Concord Image #F3868

The typical dress of the unskilled slave woman included: a head wrap, long apron, brogan shoes and a simple one-piece dress made from cotton fabric. On southern plantations, cotton fabric was homespun. It was dyed with solutions of plant leaves, plant fibers or soaked leather solutions. When ready-made clothing was store-bought (or made by hired seamstresses, the plantation wives or overseers' wives), the fabric was usually in solid colors, striped, checked or plaid and sometimes, covered with small figures or dots. Slaves received jackets and undergarments in small allotments twice a year, usually around Christmas time. Observation of women in slave dresses in 1860 photographs revealed that most dresses were patterned in the same simple style with plain waists, buttons in the center front opening of the waist, long sleeves and gathered skirts. (The term "waist," seemed to have been the common name for "bodice.")

What They Wore: The "People of Color" During The Civil War

CONTRABANDS AT FOLLIE'S FARM

CONTRABANDS AT FOLLIE'S FARM
Mass. Commandery Military Order of the Loyal Legion and USAMHI

Fig. 37. Fugitive slaves became known as "contrabands" when they left the plantations to follow the Union soldiers. Although they had become free, they had fears of an uncertain future. Their clothing is representative of the clothing worn by most slaves. (The children are without shoes.)

Chapter 4
The Slave Seamstress

It is easy to wonder and question how fabric was acquired and clothing constructed in both the North and South during the years of the Civil War. This is especially a topic of interest for the states affected by the Federal naval blockade of southern ports. Ships were forbidden from carrying goods into southern ports. This blockade caused a shortage of clothing, blankets and bandages. Most textile mills were located in northern states. Therefore, acquiring fabric and clothing was not as large a problem there. However, the decrease in cotton production in the South reduced the amount of cotton available for the mills. By the time of the Civil War, a few mills had begun operation in the South. Unlike in northern cities, there were large southern plantations with a labor force of hundreds of slaves who had to be clothed. The number of textile mills in the South increased after the war during the 1880s.

During any period of time, clothing worn by men, women, and children reflected their social status. A person's clothing mirrored the amount of wealth he possessed. Even before the turbulent Civil War years, the amount of wealth a free person of color was privileged to *acquire* depended upon whether he lived in the North or South. If a planter's family were high class, the clothing of its slaves sometimes, reflected that status. The country's population included: the poor, the elite or wealthy class of free white people, the "free people of color;" and black people in bondage. The latter group consisted of: field workers, domestic house servants, and skilled laborers. Each group dressed differently. (Illustrations in Chapters 4 and 5 show the various styles of clothing worn in each group.)

Slave Clothing, Construction and Distribution

Slave seamstresses, taught by plantation mistresses and overseers' wives, made clothing for the slaves. On large plantations, loom houses were built for spinning, weaving and clothing construction tasks. Some women worked on a task system. They were ordered to make a certain number of garments each day. Reported on one plantation, "Sarah has made this year in May, 3 pairs of mens pantaloons in a day--and made well also 3 dresses for women. Her task is 2 1/2 pairs of pants or 2 1/2 chemises or two dresses for women. Jenny Young makes 2 pr pants and shirts or makes 2 chemises or 2 dresses for women" (1,p.17)

On other plantations and small farms, each slave family received a specific yardage of cloth, thread and buttons and was held responsible for making clothes for that family. In this case, slave clothing was sewn after all other chores were finished, usually at night. Field hand slaves especially were not well-clothed which resulted in ill health.

Inadequate clothing and long working hours with meager food allowances made the life of field hand slaves extremely difficult.

Urban slaves, those who worked in cities as skilled laborers or domestics, fared better than those on farms. They had a healthier diet, were better dressed and lived in more comfortable houses.

On many farms, planters' wives made all the slave clothing or the sewing process was divided: the plantation mistress cut the fabric while slave women did the sewing. Sometimes, planters hired seamstresses to make the clothing for his family and slaves. Sewing was done by hand until the invention of sewing machines. Singer Sewing machines were in use in the 1850's. Wealthy planters who owned large plantations probably purchased the machines and ready-made clothing for their slaves.

Slave clothing was made from cheap "Nigger cloth" or osnaburg which in the 17th Century came from textile mills in England. Runaway slave newspaper ads published as early as 1775 described slave clothing as having been made from osnaburg. The cloth was coarse, tough, and in an off-white or beige color. Slaves complained bitterly about the scratchy irritation of the cloth on the skin. To vary colors, they dyed the cloth in solutions made from indigo or other plant leaves, berries and soaked leather solutions.

By the time of the Civil War, fabric from a few American mills was made of silk, wool, and cotton. Fabric patterns were plaid, polka dot, checked, and striped in a variety of colors. Before the war, slave holders could purchase ready-made clothing for slaves. White women seamstresses in northern cities received pre-cut cloth and were employed to make slave clothing in their homes for store owners. Their pay was very low and some had to depend upon charity to manage their livelihood.

Clothing allotments were distributed every spring and fall. James H. Hammond's plantation manual described the clothing allowance that masters commonly provided: "Each man gets in the fall 2 shirts of cotton drilling, a pair of woolen pants and a woolen jacket. In the spring 2 shirts of cotton shirting and 2 pr of cotton pants....Each woman gets in the fall 6 yds of woolen cloth, 6 yds of cotton drilling and a needle, skein of thread and 1/2 dozen buttons. In the spring 6 yds of cotton shirting and 6 yds of cotton cloth similar to that for men's pants, needle thread and buttons.

Slave Seamstress

Fig. 38. Crocheted Cape.

"Each worker gets a stout pr. of shoes every fall and a heavy blanket every third year. Some masters also gave socks and wool caps to the men, stockings and sunbonnets or kerchiefs to the women." (2, p.291)

For children, their clothing allowances were about the same: two long loose fitting shirts each fall and spring, but children did not receive shoes at any time. Boys up to the age of eight or twelve wore one-piece shirttails that reached below their knees. In the winter, they were given britches. Women's dresses were made in one-piece, with plain bodices; approximately four to six buttons sewn down the front opening from the neck to the natural waistline; sleeves were long and gathered at shoulder seams; no collars were sewn on; skirts were gathered at the waistline and long reaching to or near the ankles. Women wore long aprons daily.

Fig. 39. Reenactor Joyce Booker as a Slave Seamstress

Adult slaves went barefoot because the "brogan" shoes did not fit and were painful to wear. Adults received hats and coats as the weather required. Although poorly clothed, slaves took pride in their appearance. Clothing was washed once each week, hair was combed on the weekend and they dressed as well as they could on Sundays.

Among field slaves, only drivers (black overseers) received extra and slightly better clothing. Skilled slaves, hired out to others, dressed better as they were able to use some of their earnings for themselves. House slave servants were better housed, clothed and fed. Hand-me-

Slave Seamstress

Fig. 40. House servants received hand-me-down clothing from the plantation mistress. *Left to right,* Reenactors Sharon R. Yates and Mary J. Fears.

down clothing was given to them from the planter and his wife. Written accounts of travelers to southern plantations reported that planters usually clothed house servants, butlers, and coachmen very lavishly to demonstrate their wealth and social standing.

If an ad for the sale of a female seamstress described her as "a likely seamstress," it meant that she was highly skilled as a seamstress, and was one who was efficient in spinning, weaving, knitting and crocheting. On some plantations, all genders, young and old, did needle work. Young girls and women were trained to make quilts. Division of labor on plantations varied.

The largest production of textiles was done with slave labor. However, a large amount of fabric for slave garments was produced in northern factories. Cloth was most often homespun from cotton fibers and hand-woven on plantations. Slaves did the spinning, weaving, dyeing and construction of most garments worn by those in bondage. Some slaves developed expertise in sewing skills and they, like Elizabeth Keckley used the income from those skills to purchase their freedom.

---

1. Fry, Gladys-Marie. Stitched From The Soul, Slave Quilts From the Ante-Bellum South. NY: Dutton Studio Books, 1990.

2. Stamp, Kenneth M. The Peculiar Institution, Slavery in the Ante-Bellum South. NY: Alfred A. Knopf, 1965.

Clothing of "Free People of Color"

Clothing worn by "free people of color" during the Civil War years, in all probability, can be attributed to *how* they became free. Had they been born into families of wealth within free states as Charlotte Forten, clothing would have been affordable and representative of the most stylish apparel available. Charlotte, the granddaughter of James Forten, a wealthy black man who owned a very successful business, was born free. She would have dressed appropriately as a free person and a teacher. Mrs. James Babcock, a free black, had a bakery business in Salem, Massachusetts and could choose to dress as much in stylish fashions as desired. (See page 10.)

On the other hand, if a fugitive slave had fled with only the slave clothing upon his back, and had become free by a successful escape, his clothing would consist of whatever some benevolent donor could afford to give him until he gained employment. In escape accounts published as "slave narratives" barely any explanation of clothing received and worn later is mentioned.

"Free people of color" living in slave holding states would have fared better economically than those in bondage. Their clothing, based upon current styles, would have represented whatever they could have afforded. Since these persons were free as a result of either being manumitted by law or by the will of a former slave master or was fortunate enough to have purchased their freedom, their clothing would have depended upon their sources of income. However, since they lived in close proximity to their slave brethren, their lives were extremely restricted. They had to remain extremely vigilant in order to obey all laws pertaining to their behavior or be thrust back into slavery. Under these strenuous living conditions, simply by conjecture, elaborate expensive clothing was not their primary interest. Since they were so highly victimized by their free status as black people, and their means of employment was restricted, it remains doubtful that they dressed as well as free persons of color in non-slaving holding states.

Since reenacting in Civil War events requires wearing appropriate attire, reenactors must know where to look to become familiar with clothing styles of the Civil War era. Clothing styles of men, women and teens of that time period are pictured in "Who Wore What? Women's Wear, 1861-1865 by Juanita Leisch (Gettysburg: Thomas Publications, 1995). Many of the photographs were taken in photography studios.

For the styles of younger children, see Heidi Marsh's book, What Children Wore (Or Wished They Could) In The Era Of The Hoop. It is an excellent guide. It contains a collection of children's clothing styles with quotes from 1860s fashion magazines: *Godey's Lady's Book and Magazine, Peterson's Magazine, Arthur's Home Magazine, and Lady's Friend.* It is an authentic guide for children's clothing in the 1860s. However, if these books are not readily available, other

TEENAGE NURSE

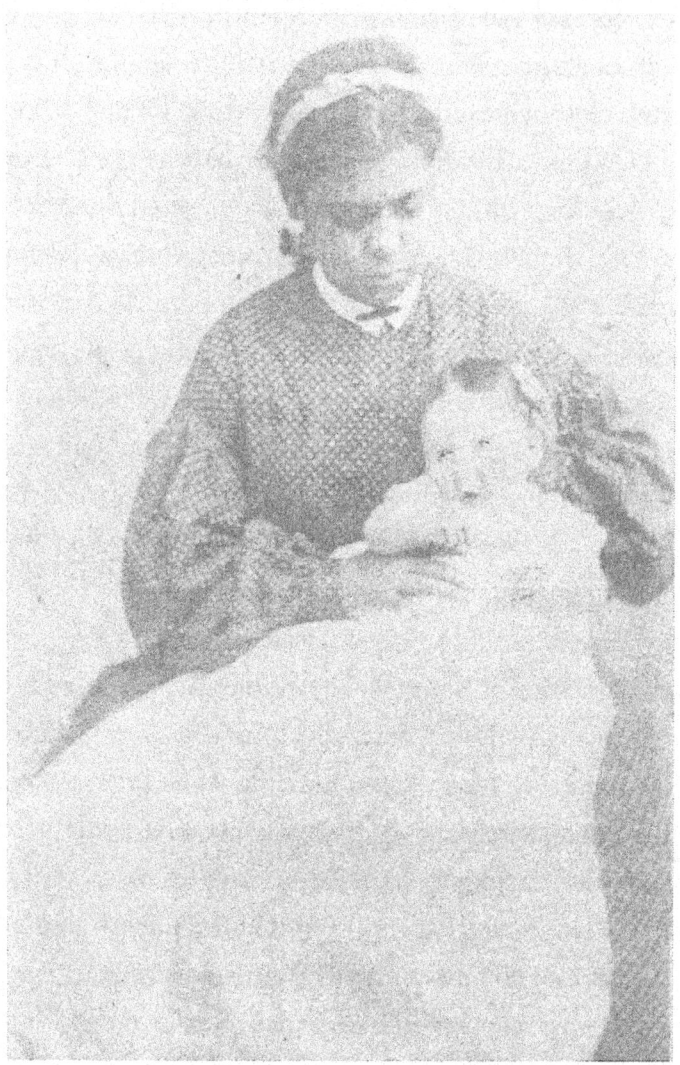

Fig. 41. Aunt Lizzie
Courtesy, Valentine Museum

    This unidentified teenage nurse is dressed well because she is a domestic "house servant." Slaves who worked in the slave master's homes were given better clothing. She is wearing a stylish polka dot dress with a narrow white cotton collar, and a pin to clasp it. The dress has dropped shoulder seams attached to wide sleeves. Her hair has the usual center part with a ribbon tied across it.

Clothing of "Free People of Color"

Fig. 42. Child's Dress with Cape

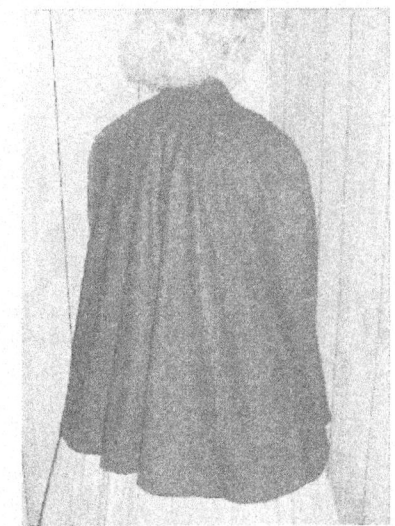

Fig. 43. Wool Cape. Capes and shawls were favorite wraps. Long cloaks required many yards of fabric to cover the hoops.

titles listed in the bibliography following this chapter can be found in most public libraries and book stores.

Persons beginning the hobby of reenacting will find it unnecessary to select the most expensive, lavishly adorned clothing. Civilians worked, did household chores and dressed casually in everyday clothing as people today. The requirement is authenticity. Unlike the dresses of slave women, the dresses of free people of color during the ante-bellum years were not all made alike.

Just as in modern times, a basic style of dress may be described. Added trimmings, like gathered fringed edgings made from the dress fabric and crocheted lace in different sizes and colors placed in appropriate arrangements, can vary the appearance of the basic dress to create the 1860s look. Men, women and children's clothing can be purchased or ordered from sutlers at Civil War reenactments or they can be made. If a decision is made to purchase the clothing, the buyers should be aware of the colors and types of fabric that were available during the time period in order not to be mislead into the purchase of something inappropriate.

To inspire maximum participation by novice reenactors, dresses that are economical, thus simply made are illustrated and suggested in this guide. Sometimes, during visits to thrift stores, persons may be able to find suitable clothing items that can be altered to appear appropriate in style. Clothing worn by reenactors should be historically accurate by being made as similar as possible to those seen in historic photographs of the period. If reenacting in the role of a specific character, the clothing should be consistent with the occupation of that individual.

Clothing of "Free People of Color"

ACCESSORIES

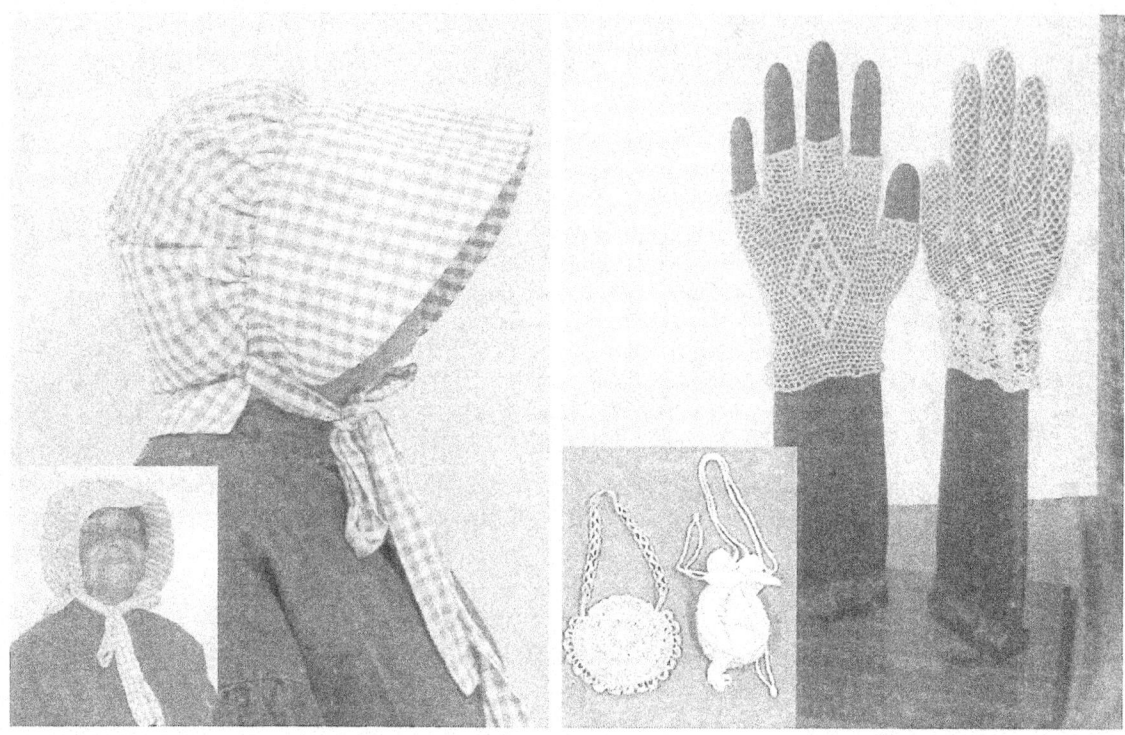

Fig. 44a. Reenactor Edith Jackson in a Bonnet

Fig. 44b. Purses and Gloves

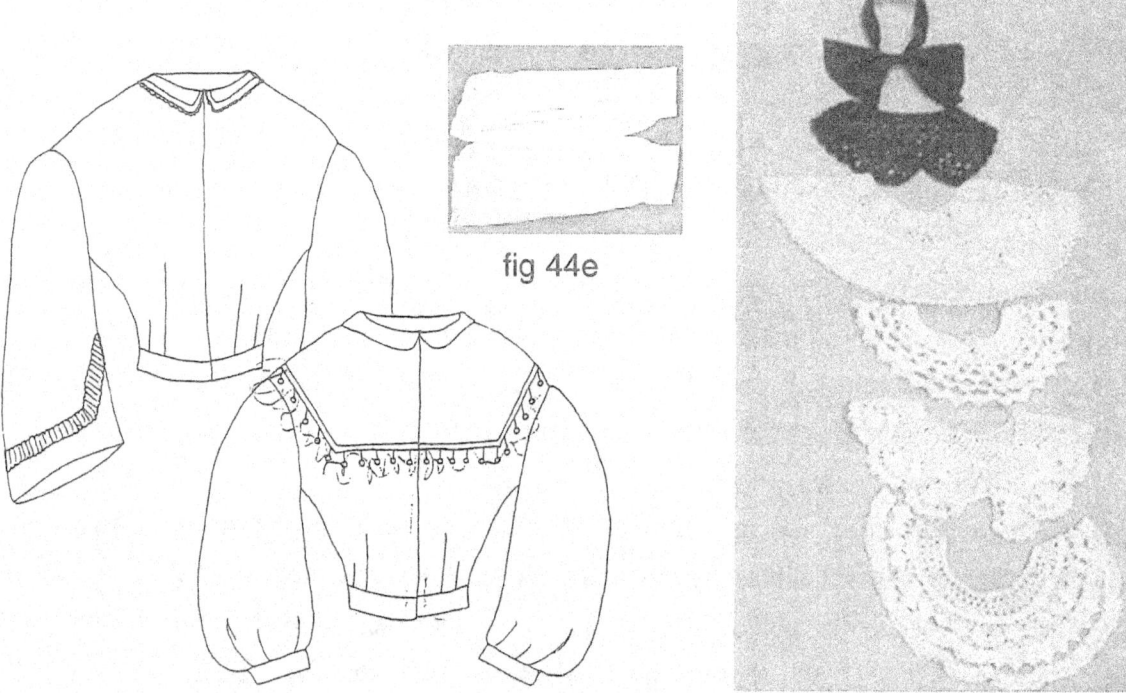

Fig. 44c. Garibaldi Blouse

fig 44e

Fig. 44d. Crocheted collars

Clothing of "Free People of Color"

The following is a description of the 1860s *look* of clothing to be worn by reenactors representative of "free persons of color." Photographs and drawn illustrations on the pages that follow clarify descriptions of the various clothing items.

Skirts

Whether on a one-piece dress, or separate to be worn with a blouse, skirts were fully gathered at the waist and long, reaching at least four inches from the floor. On teens, the dress length was shorter, a few inches above the ankle.

Bodice

The bodice touched the natural waistline. Dresses were worn with or without belts. Older women did not wear belts. Trimmings on the bodice formed a "Y" or "V" or the waist was described as "round." Most dress bodices had the dropped sleeves as were made in garibaldi blouses.

Sleeves

Women's dresses had long sleeves, puffed at the elbow. Detachable sleeves were made from white fabric or the matching fabric of the dress. Sleeves on teen dresses were short. Some dresses had bolero tops with wide pagoda styled sleeves. Detachable sleeves or the end of blouse sleeves could be seen within the wide opening of the pagoda sleeves.

Necklines and collars

Except for ball gowns, the necklines were close to the neck or "jewel" type. Gathered lace was often sewn inside around the neck opening. Collars were crocheted or made with white or light colored cloth, detachable and narrow, one and a half inches wide. Older women wore wider collars. not more than four inches in width. Some dresses had no collars. Dress collars and cuffs were detachable. A decorative pin, brooch or ribbon bow was worn in the center of the collar. Teen dresses had lower necklines.

Garibaldi Blouses (with cuff sleeves)

Seams which attached long sleeves to the garibaldi blouses were about two inches below the usual shoulder seam and gathered at that seam. The bodice of dresses had the same placement of sleeve seams. Button holes were sewn down the center front of blouses.

Hairstyles

Women's hairstyles in 1860s' photographs showed women's hair parted in the center of the forehead, lying flat on top, pulled back covering the ears, and clustered in curls at the back of the head. In some photographs, the hair did not cover the ears.

Crocheted snoods or hair nets sometimes covered the hair clustered at the back.

Clothing of "Free People of Color"

Fig. 45a. 1860s Hair Style
(with hanging style of jewelry)

Fig. 45b. 1860s Velvet Trimmed Hat

Fig. 45c. 1860s Hat Tilted
Down Towards the Forehead

Fig. 45d. Crocheted Collar, Jewelry
and Hair Style of the 1860s

Trimmings

Lace trimmings were added to bodices, sleeves and skirts or dresses in plain or solid colors. Civil War photographs show the placement of trimmings. They were sewn in three or four rows near the bottom of the skirt and arranged on bodices and sleeves.

Fabric

Fabric designs included plaids, polka dots, stripes, checks, geometric prints or small flowers. The material most often used was cotton, but wool, silk and linen cloth were also available. Younger women's dresses may have used two contrasting pieces of fabric for the bodice and skirt.

Under garments

Wearing a corset and a hoop beneath the skirt is very necessary to acquire the look of a petite waistline and the desired appearance of women during the Civil War era.. Hoops, corsets, chemises, slips, drawers with open seams in the crotch (for ease in using the toilet when wearing the wide hoops) and stockings are available from sutlers at Civil War reenactments or they can be ordered. However, if a reenactor desires to appear as wearing a "day dress" the hoop can be omitted. The wearing of the remaining under garments are optional. Wide crinoline slips may be worn in place of a hoop.

Accessories

Hats, purses, crocheted and cloth gloves, shoes, stockings, fans, jewelry, and parasols are all accessories available from sutlers. Except for the shoes and white stockings, all accessories listed are optional or may be acquired gradually. "Brogan" type shoes similar in style to those of the Civil War era can be found in shoe stores or thrift shops. Mitts and open-fingered gloves were not always worn at that time. Jewelry was sometimes worn attached to belts. A reenactor should always begin with a basic correctly styled outfit consisting of the dress, stockings and shoes. Sutlers carry a wide selection of accessory items. They are the best sources for hats.

Capes and Shawls

Women wore capes of various lengths for warmth in cold weather, also cloaks and coats. However, capes for the reenactor would be the easiest to acquire as they are less expensive. They can be purchased or ordered from sutlers or easily made since they have no sleeves, only openings for the arms. Capes were made long and full to hang from the neck and loosely over the hooped dresses. Capes made from wool fabric are a welcomed part of the reenactor's outfit on cool mornings and evenings when spending nights at the reenactment camp. Shawls were made from knitted fabric both with and without fringes. They were also made from fabric with designs in them.

Clothing of "Free People of Color"

MALE "FREE PERSONS OF COLOR"

Fig. 46. Suit style of the 1860s.
Collection of Deborah Cooney

Fig. 47. Rev. John Jasper, a Preacher.*
Courtesy of Sixth Mt. Zion Baptist Church, Richmond, VA

Men's Civilian Clothing of the 1860s

Men wore suits made from wool fabric, either plain or trimmed with braid-bound edges and brass buttons, with matching vests and white small-collared shirts and narrow neck bows. A gold watch chain hung from a vest buttonhole may have been added. Cotton shirts were white or beige in color or made with colored striped or plaid fabric. Sutlers at Civil War reenactment sites carry men's ready-made clothing and suit fabric of the period. Other items include: muslin cotton shirts, suspenders, trousers, vests, ties, belts, socks and shoes. (See ads at the end of the text.)

*Rev. John Jasper is suggested as a character for a civilian reenacting role. Jasper, the last of 24 children, was born a slave in Fluvanna County on 4 July 1812. In 1825, he left the plantation and came to Richmond, VA to work as an industrial slave. He was taught how to read by a fellow slave. After his conversion experience, he became a preacher. In September 1867, he organized the Sixth Mt. Zion Baptist church in a former Confederate stable on Brown's Island. The church is a historic landmark in Richmond. Rev. Jasper, credited for being the first black man to organize a church in post-Civil War times, became nationally known for his unique style of delivering sermons. (See also photographs of Frederick Douglass for male suit styles.)

CLOTHING STYLES

Fig. 48.

Fig. 49

Fig. 48. **Janome Ward**
Courtesy of Helena Melicent Remy

This lady is dressed in stylish fashion. She is wearing a solid color one-piece dress or a matching skirt and blouse. She is without gloves and a snood (hair net) as women did not always wear them during the Civil War period. When hair nets were worn, they were dark. Hair styles were consistently the same, with a center part and combed to the back of the head. Her dress has the fan or "Y" bodice formed by the trimming. The skirt is gathered at the waist. As with most dresses, it has a small white collar and clasp used for pinning it together.

Fig. 49. **Mother with One Boy**
Library of Congress USZ62-132210

The clothing of this woman and boy suggests that they are members of a "free family." The striped and trimmed Zouave jacket on the boy has pockets or imitation pockets. His shirt is white with cuffs or ruffles. The woman's dress is belted and has the usual small white collar and pin clasp. The waist of the dress is gathered at the front forming the fitted "V" shaped bodice. Another common shape of an 1860s dress bodice is gathered in front and described as an "O" bodice. Even though footwear is not shown, research revealed that shoe heels in the 1860s had a one to one and a half inch height. They were wide across the toes. Small boots laced up the front over buttons.

Fig. 50. JANE PATTERSON
A "Free Woman of Color"
Courtesy of Oberlin College

Miss Jane Patterson, an honor student, was the first black graduate to receive a Bachelor of Science Degree from Oberlin College in 1862. She is pictured in a garibaldi shirt of black or red wool. Her dropped full sleeves are of the extreme "elbow style." The gathered skirt, worn over a hoop, was probably made from black and white wool checked fabric. Rows of silk trimming sewn around and above the hem, add to its beauty. As in most dresses of the era, white lace is crimped around the neckline. She is wearing a dark colored corded belt.

    For reenactors in the role of "free persons of color," skirt and blouse sets may be made similarly to this one from either wool or cotton fabric. For matching skirt and waist sets, narrow white cotton lace may be sewn into the narrow neck bands and topped with a neck ribbon or a brooch.. An alternative is to make a collarless one-piece dress with the Garibaldi-type blouse and add a detachable small white cotton collar with a one and a half inch width. Sew five or six buttons down the front opening of the blouse. Make the skirt of the dress very full to cover a hoop. Skirt and blouse sets were popular in the 1860s for casual wear.
See Fig. 62, page 105. Rows of lace (with the appearance of crochet) may be sewn in decorative arrangements on skirts, sleeves, and waists to make a more beautiful outfit.

FABRIC PATTERNS

FABRIC

The fabric patterns on the preceding page include: plaids, stripes, polka dots, checks and a solid white piece. These fabric patterns may be used by Civil War reenactors as a guide for fabric selection. By the time of the Civil War, textile mills manufactured cloth from cotton, wool, linen and silk fibers in a variety of colors and weaves. Fabric was commercially available in stores. However, after the Union blockade of Southern ports, fabric was scarce in some areas

Silk was the most expensive fabric. Since cotton fabric was the least expensive, most women's dresses were made from cotton. 1860s photographs show fabric designs with small dots, flowers and geometric figures on a solid background. Textile mills created some fabric designs, not only with colors, but with variations in the weave. Some fabric in the 1860s even had a shiny texture similar to polished cotton and taffeta. Wool fabric was used in women's dresses and men's clothing. Sutlers at Civil War reenactments sell period fabric in appropriate colors.

Beginning in the 1850s, chemical dyes were used by textile mills to make fabric in various colors and hues. The colors of fabric in quilts made before and around the years of the Civil War may be used as a guide to reenactors when considering colors of fabric to purchase. Gladys-Marie Fry's <u>Stitched from the Soul, Slave Quilts from the Ante-Bellum South</u> (NY: Dutton Studio Books, 1990) features color photographs of slave-made quilts. None of the quilts in Fry's book included quilt blocks made from fabric with large flowers or extremely large designs. The color purple does not appear in any of the slave quilts. The quilts shown had fabric in the basic colors and hues: dark red, orange, blue, green, yellow, black, gray, brown, white and beige. The slave quilts were pieced with scraps from: solid color cloth, striped, plaid and checked fabric. Some quilt pieces contained small dots on solid backgrounds in a variety of colors.

Juanita Leisch shows many photographs in <u>Who Wore What, Women's Wear, 1861-1865</u> (Gettysburg, PA: Thomas Publications, 1995) as illustrations with descriptions of the fabric in women's clothing. The books by these two authors, Fry and Leisch, are suggested for purchase and reference sources.

Osnaburg

Osnaburg was a coarse cream or off-white colored fabric made from cotton fibers for slave clothing It was manufactured in Northern and European textile mills. On some plantations, water-powered mills were built to supply coarse cloth for slave clothing. It had the appearance of today's unbleached muslin. To change the boring color, plantation slaves dyed the fabric using solutions made from various plant fibers.

BOYS' 1860s STYLE CLOTHING

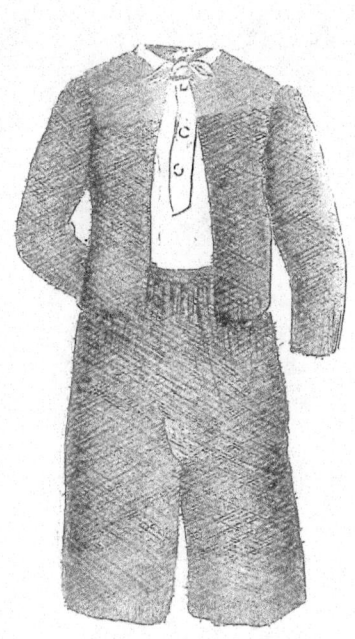

Fig. 51a. A Small Boy's Suit
A boy in a "free family" could wear a suit like this one. It included: a jacket, shirt, tied ribbon neck bow, vest, and long trousers. Suit fabric: wool, checked or solid dark color.

Fig. 51b. A Photograph of a "Contraband"
He is wearing a cap, shirt, vest, and trousers with a cloth tied as a belt. (Usually cloth suspenders were worn by boys and men.)

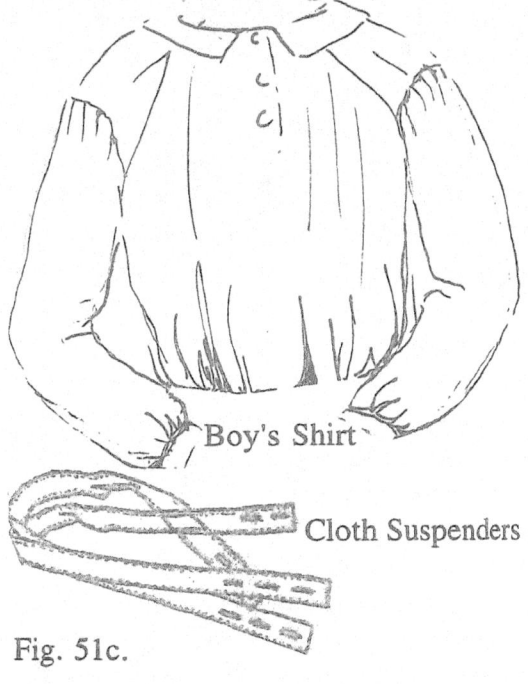

Boy's Shirt

Cloth Suspenders

Fig. 51c.

Trousers were made without gathers or pleats at the waist band. Two wooden buttons were added to the front and back of the waist band for the suspenders.

Fig. 51d. Boy's Shirt and Trousers

GIRLS' 1860s STYLE CLOTHING

Fig. 52a. Front view of slave girl's dress. (Reenactors should wear shoes with covered toes.)

Fig. 52b. Back view of slave girl's dress. Slave children did not receive shoes to wear.

Fig. 52c. Dress for a "free girl of color." Shoes were the brogan type.

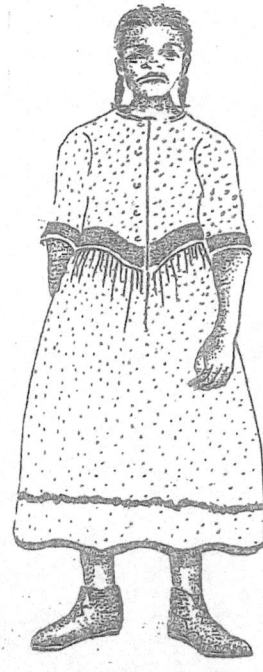

Fig. 52d. Artist's drawing of a dress made by an unknown slave from the scraps of a bedspread.

YOUNG REENACTORS

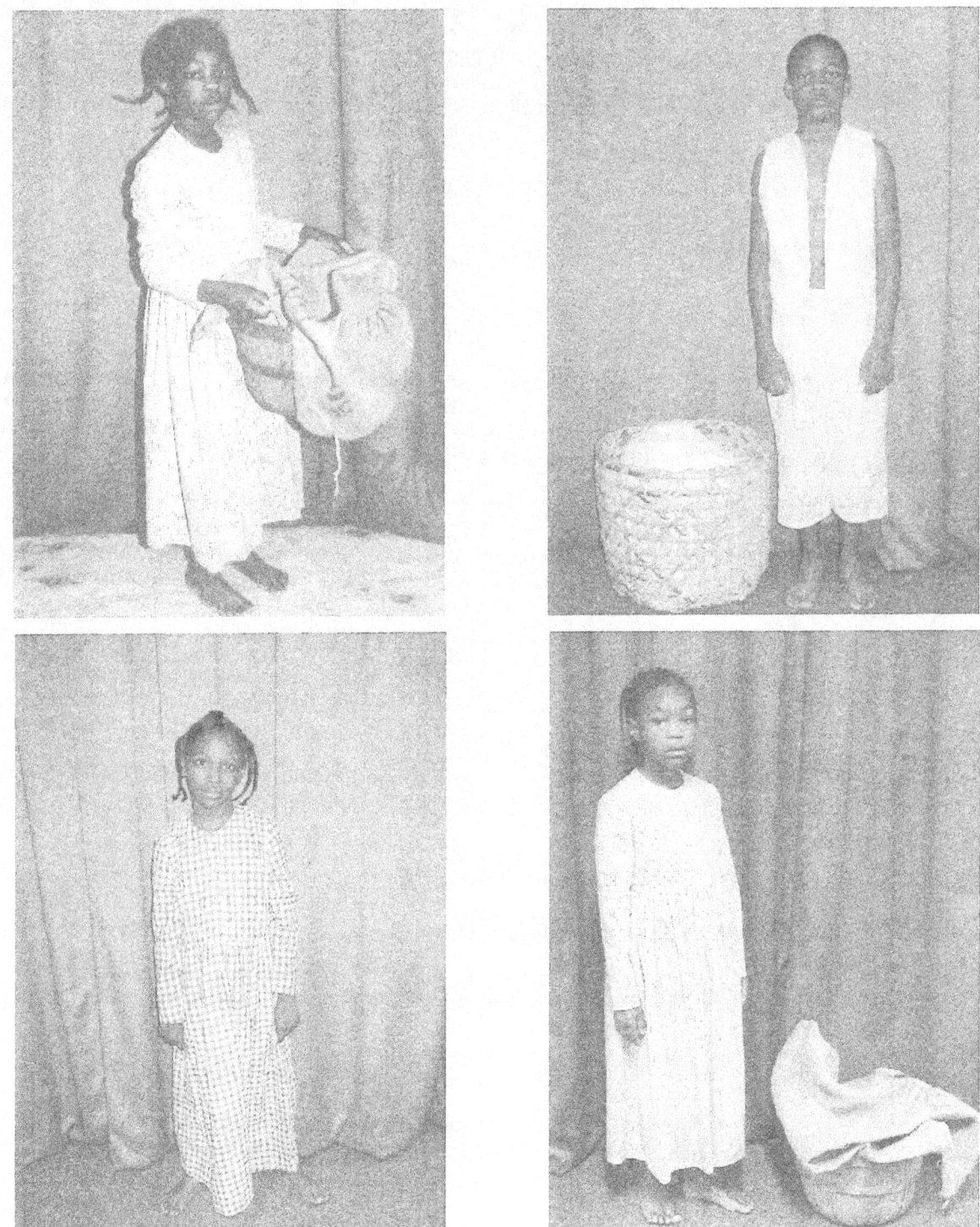

Fig. 53. REENACTORS AS SLAVE CHILDREN
Top, left to right: Carah Young and Michael Frazier (For shirt, see Fig. 51c.)
Bottom, left to right: Zaporah Frazier and Carah Young

Bibliography
Civil War Clothing Styles for "People of Color"

Some titles include photographs depicting clothing of field slaves, house servants, and "free people of color." They are informative for civilian reenactors.

Blum, Stella, Editor. <u>Fashions and Costumes from Godey's Lady's Book</u>. NY: Dover Publications, 1985.

Civil War Ladies: <u>Fashions and Needle-Arts of the Early 1860's.</u> R.L. Shep, Box 668, Mendocino, CA 95460.

Clinton, Catherine. <u>The Plantation Mistress, Woman's World In The old South.</u> NY: Pantheon Books, 1982.
    The chapter, "Slave of Slaves." discusses in detail the many slave-related tasks assigned to the plantation mistress like the production of clothing for her husband's slaves. The author used letters, journals, diaries, and other documents written by and about plantation women as reference sources for her text.

Faust, Drew Gilpin. <u>Mothers of Invention, Women of the Slaveholding South in the American Civil War.</u> Chapel Hill, NC: Univ. of North Carolina Press, 1996.
    The author discusses the plight of southern plantation women after their husbands and sons went off to fight in the Civil War. Southern women were left with new responsibilities which involved the challenge of managing their slaves.

Fry, Gladys-Marie, Ph.D. <u>Stitched From the Soul, Slave Quilts from the Ante-Bellum South.</u> NY: Dutton Bks., 1990.
    Includes photographs of slaves, slave dwellings, and excerpts from slave narratives which explain slave-clothing construction and distribution, life of the slave seamstress, quilting and slave life on plantations.

Genovese, Eugene D. <u>Roll Jordan Roll, The World The Slaves Made.</u> NY: Vintage Bks. 1974.
    The author covers a range of topics including "Life in the Big House," "Men of Skill," "Free Negroes," and "Clothes Make the Man and the Woman."

Leisch, Juanita. <u>Who Wore What? Women's Wear 1861-1865.</u> Gettysburg, PA: Thomas Publications, 1995.
    This book is completely filled with pages of 1860s photographs and detailed explanations on each piece of women's wearing apparel worn during the Civil War period. It is an excellent guide for women's wear during the 1860s.

Marsh, Heidi. <u>What Children Wore (Or Wished They Could) In The Era Of The Hoop.</u>
    Greenville, CA., 1993. The book contains a vast collection of children's clothing with quotes from 1860's fashion magazines: *Godey's Lady's Book and Magazine, Peterson's Magazine, Arthur's Home Magazine,* and *Lady's Friend.* It is an authentic guide for children's clothing in the 1860s.

McKissack, Patricia and Frederick McKissack. <u>Christmas in the Big House, Christmas in the Quarters.</u> NY: Scholastic, 1994.
    McKissack describes slave Christmas celebrations on the plantation. Pages 27 and 51 show the slave dress of female and male adult slaves. Pages 31 and 39 show the dresses of a slave girl, and page 59 shows the clothing of a slave boy. Buttons were wooden. This is an excellent informational book for readers of all ages.

Bibliography
Civil War Clothing Styles for "People of Color"

Miller, Randall M. and John David Smith, Editors. <u>Dictionary of Afro-American Slavery.</u> NY: Greenwood Press, 1988.
    The authors include a detailed discussion on the making and distribution of slave clothing.

Mohr, Clarence L. <u>On The Threshold of Freedom.</u> Athens, GA: Univ. of Georgia Press, 1986.
    Chapter titles: "Black Georgians" and "The Union War Effort, 1861-1865." A change was made in the clothing worn by slaves on the Sea Islands of the South Carolina coast and in coastal Georgia after the Union's capture of Port Royal, SC in November 1861. All plantation owners fled abandoning their homes. Their slaves became free and "appropriated their mistress' wearing apparel while the men rioted over their master's wine." Thus the freed slaves began to dress as their former mistresses in the styles of free people during the years of the Civil War.

Stamp, Kenneth M. <u>The Peculiar Institution, Slavery in the Ante-Bellum South.</u> NY: Alfred A. Knopf, 1965.
    This author's work is recognized as an accurate overview of slavery. Within its chapters, all phases of the system are discussed. The clothing of both slaves and "free persons of color" are presented.

Thompson, Kathleen. <u>The Face of Our Past, Images of Black Women from Colonial America to the Present.</u> Bloomington, IN: Indiana Univ. Press, 1999.
    A book of photographs which will aid black women reenactors in selecting appropriate clothing styles for the Civil War era. Request to see it at public libraries and book stores.

Tobin, Jacqueline and Raymond Dobard. <u>Hidden in Plain View, A Secret Story of Quilts and the Underground Railroad.</u> NY: Anchor Bks., 2000.

Varhola, Michael J. <u>Everyday Life During the Civil War, A Guide for Writers, Students and Historians.</u> Cincinnati, OH: Writer's Digest Bks., 1999.
Includes the chapter, "Clothing and Other Dry Goods." Clothing illustrated was worn by all *free* people during the Civil War era. Excellent guide for reenactors.

MAKING DO WITH WHAT YOU HAVE

Fig. 54a. Display of Male Slave Clothing.

Fig. 54b. Joel Fears, Jr.

Reenactor Joel Fears, Jr. wears an acceptable outfit to represent male slave clothing.

With an ordinary male cotton shirt made from either striped or plaid fabric, anyone can make the following adjustments: remove the collar and leave the band standing; remove pockets; stitch down the front opening beginning with the fifth button; remove remaining four buttons and sew on four wooden buttons. If a shirt is used that is much too large, then both sides of the front can be stitched together without leaving the old button holes showing.

For the trousers, select a beige cotton pair with as few pockets as possible. Cover back pockets with cloth patches. Remove all belt loops. Sew two wooden buttons on the front and back waist band. Use two pieces of 1-to-2 inch wide strips of muslin or osnaburg fabric for the suspenders. Sew wooden buttons and buttonholes on the placket. (Zippers were not available.)

Make or purchase a vest with the roll down collar as shown at the top of the rack. The modern vest on the bottom is *not* correct for the period. Purchase a pair of brogan shoes, and the outfit is complete.

Chapter 5
What to Wear: Making Do with What You Have

Shakespeare wrote in *Romeo and Juliet,* "That which we call a rose, by any other name would smell as sweet."[1] No matter what side slaves served in the Civil War, whether they went with their masters as "body servants;" or were "impressed" into the service of the Confederacy; or whether they fled into Union lines as "contrabands;" on either side, they performed the same. They did the hard work in menial tasks. It was all non-combat service. They were both skilled and unskilled as laborers. However, all dug up and packed down, cooked and cleaned; washed and ironed, drove and were driven to handle the wagons as teamsters; and labored without ceasing, in whatever task assigned on both sides.

Nevertheless, in contrast to those on the Confederate side, thousands of young male former slaves who escaped and became "contrabands" in the Union forces, eventually were *enlisted* in the Federal army or navy as Union soldiers or sailors. In the Confederacy, historians report that a number of slave body servants and "free people of color" were clad and photographed in uniforms but Confederate military records do not show *factual* enlistments. (See Appendix E, Marlboro Jones, Body Servant.)

Even so, every slave on both sides left his loved ones back home on plantations within the chinked walls of slave cabins. Other families were left within the better houses of the fortunate few "free people of color" throughout the war years. Those home folk sent soft murmurs of prayers ascending with the belief that a Union victory would bring freedom to every slave household. However, many slave wives and children did not remain back home on plantations. The wives followed their husbands into Union camps and became "slave female contrabands." This situation created another role for female reenactors to learn about for interpreting Civil War experiences. The Museum of the Confederacy published details about the Civil War experiences of this "Species of Property."[2] (See Appendix F, Female Contrabands.)

Female Contrabands

Slave women with their children fled as fugitives, became contrabands, and attached themselves to Union troops to grasp freedom for themselves. In contrast to the acceptance of slave men into Union ranks, female slave contrabands and their children, which numbered in the thousands, provoked verbal outrage, and hostility from Union soldiers. Even though many women were assigned tasks as cooks and washerwomen for the soldiers, their vast numbers created problems. One Union soldier described their presence as an "evil" burden.

The contraband policy, when first employed by Union General Benjamin Butler, was not intended to include women and children. As their presence reached monumental numbers, they became like the "families of soldiers needing food and housing." They were housed in makeshift shanties near Union camps. But even there for protection, besides the unwelcomed attention of some soldiers, the women and children risked danger of being recaptured by slave masters. The women who fled the Southern plantations experienced sad consequences, but they, by fleeing slavery, contributed to its final destruction.

In spite of Lincoln's efforts to keep the war's objective focused on restoring the Union, the actions of slave fugitives compelled attention to the slavery issue and made it impossible to ignore. Despite the sentiment that contraband women had no place within Union lines, the promise of freedom continued to encourage flight. Another motivation that increased flight was the brutal retaliation of slave masters and mistresses upon those who did not flee to Union lines.[2] Aside from their service as cooks and washerwomen in Union camps, many female contrabands served as nurses in Union hospitals.

Reenactors may consider either the role of slaves as contrabands or other roles as "free people of color." Free black people in towns and slave families on plantations were all a part of the population. They were there and lived through it all. The Civil War reenactment scene will *be* complete with their presence. Reenactors in either role help to complete that scene. Clothing requirements to fill the role of a civilian Civil War reenactor can be as easy as "making do with what one already has," together with a few minor purchases.

To be a civilian reenactor, not representative of any specific character, is easy. All that is required is to attend a reenactment and proudly stroll around dressed in a role as a very important "living history" representative of the Civil War population. One may consider the role of a skilled person. People of color were skilled in numerous occupations: coopers, cabinetmakers, carpenters, brick masons, blacksmiths, butchers, cooks, bakers, barbers, tailors, preachers, painters, boot and shoemakers, seamstresses, nurses, midwives, teachers and in other skills.

To enhance the role, a reenactor should: read about the skill as practiced during the 1860s, become knowledgeable about how the skill was learned, make a study of the tools used, and, if possible, acquire one or more of the tools, research in books and on the internet to find names of persons who practiced the skill. Then assume that character's role to speak about and portray.

Illustrations in this chapter show how to "make do with what you have."

1. Shakespeare, William. *Romeo and Juliet.*, Act II, Scene 2, Line 43.

2. See "Female Slave Contrabands in the Civil War" in <u>A Woman's War, Southern Women, Civil War and the Confederate Legacy.</u> Edited by Edward D.C. Campbell, Jr. and Kym S. Rice. Charlottesville: Museum of the Confederacy, Richmond, 1996.

MAKING DO WITH WHAT YOU HAVE

The Dress After the Change

Fig. 55. An ordinary dress can be changed to become a "slave dress" within a matter of minutes. Select a cotton dress with a gathered skirt in a solid color, (or it may be plaid or checked) in a subdued shade. Fabric in the following colors are suggested: beige, brown, blue, or green in medium or dark shades. Purchase from a sutler at a reenactment, or make a garibaldi blouse and cover the bodice. Put on a long apron and tie it in the back. Put on a pair of brogan shoes and wear a cloth tied in the back of the head and the outfit is complete. Slave dresses of unskilled laborers were "work dresses." They were very simply made. (See Fig. 37, page 66.)

1860s DRESSES FOR TEENS

Teen Dresses

Fig. 56. Girls within "free black families" were privileged to wear dresses made in the above styles. These illustrations were based upon photographs printed in books listed in the bibliographies on pages 82 and 83. Special features: *Left*, detached undersleeves (see page 74) worn under the pagoda sleeves; *Right*, wide Swiss belt with up and downward points. Some dresses were made from silk fabric in solid colors during the 1860s.

Where to Look for What to Wear

Cost and copyright restrictions made it impossible to include in this guide many 1860s photographs of "people of color" in the clothing styles of the Civil War era, 1861-1865.

However, Civil War reenactors can view the appropriate styles of clothing to wear in books featuring photographs of slaves and "free people of color" dressed in the clothing that they wore. To be successful as a reenactor, it is absolutely necessary to visit libraries to read books for knowledge and assistance.

Listed below are four book titles with page numbers which show 1860s photographs of authentic *illustrations* of clothing. The books may be borrowed at public libraries or secured through interlibrary loans.

For photographs in slave clothing, see the following:
Severa, Joan L. Dressed for the Photographer, Ordinary Americans and Fashion, 1840-1900.
    (Kent, OH: Kent State University Press, 1995). page 290 for a slave boy's jacket (seated) and man's vest (standing).

Thompson, Kathleen and Hilary Mac Austin. The Face Of Our Past. (Bloomington, IN: Indiana
    University Press, 1999).
    pages: 130, 163, and 167 for slave women's dresses; page 40 for slave women and men's clothing. Women's dresses are made from plaids and checked fabric.

For Slave children:
    See illustrations in this text and in Patricia McKissack's Christmas in the Big House, Christmas in the Quarters. (NY: Scholastic, 1994). pages 31 and 39, only.

For photographs of the clothing of slave "house servants," see the following:
Severa, Joan L. Dressed for the Photographer, Ordinary Americans and Fashion, 1840-1900.
    (Kent, OH: Kent State University Press, 1995) pages: 218 and 281 for teenagers.

See illustrations in this text and in Patricia McKissack's Christmas in the Big House, Christmas in
    the Quarters. (NY: Scholastic, 1994). page 51 for adult male and female house servants
    See only the male's clothing on page 20. The man's vest need not have the "v" cut on the collar, make the vest straight without the "v" cut.

For photographs of the clothing of "free people of color," see the following:
Severa, Joan L. Dressed for the Photographer, Ordinary Americans and Fashion, 1840-1900.
    (Kent, OH: Kent State University Press, 1995). pages: 226, 272 and 269 for adult women.
    page 243 for details of the bodice, sleeves and collar of a female adult's 1860s style dress.
    page 244 for a simple style of a pre-teen's dress.
    page 268 for the suit style for a teen or adult male. (Use with or without the coat trimming.)
    page 269 for simple jackets for small boys.

Fry, Gladys-Marie. Stitched From The Soul, Slave Quilts From the Ante-Bellum South. (NY:
    Dutton Studio Bks., 1990). pages: 14 and 15 for a male adult shirt and suit (Observe the coat trimming.)

Wilson, Jackie Napoleon. Hidden Witness, African American Images from the Dawn of
    Photography to the Civil War. NY: St.Martin's Press, 1999.
    This book includes a collection of black photographs showing 1860s style clothing.

CIVIL WAR REENACTORS

Confederate Reenactors

Union Reenactors

Fig. 57. Confederate and Union Reenactors at the 2003 Battle of Olustee Reenactment
The Civil War Battle of Olustee was fought February 20, 1864 at Olustee, a town located near Lake City, Florida.

Why Reenact About "People of Color" At Civil War Reenactments

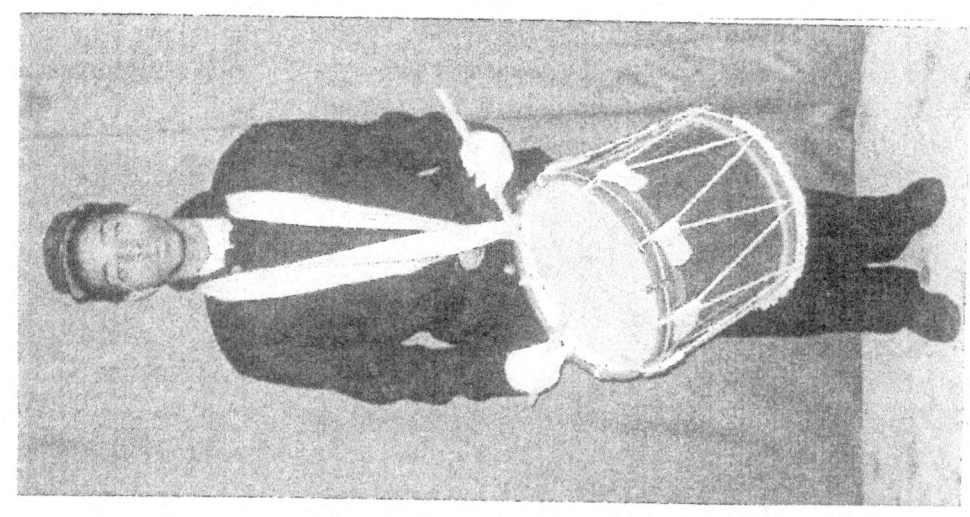

Fig.59. Reenactor Jesus Laino uniformed as Jackson, the Drummer Boy.

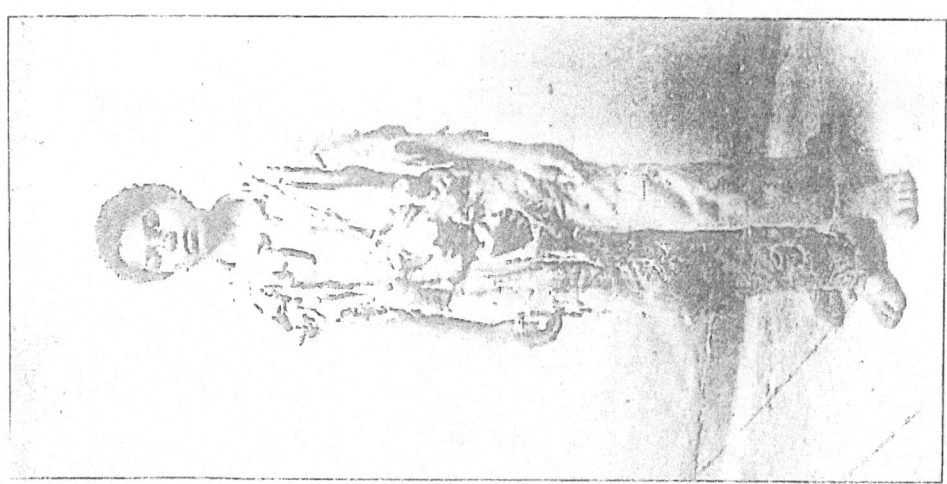
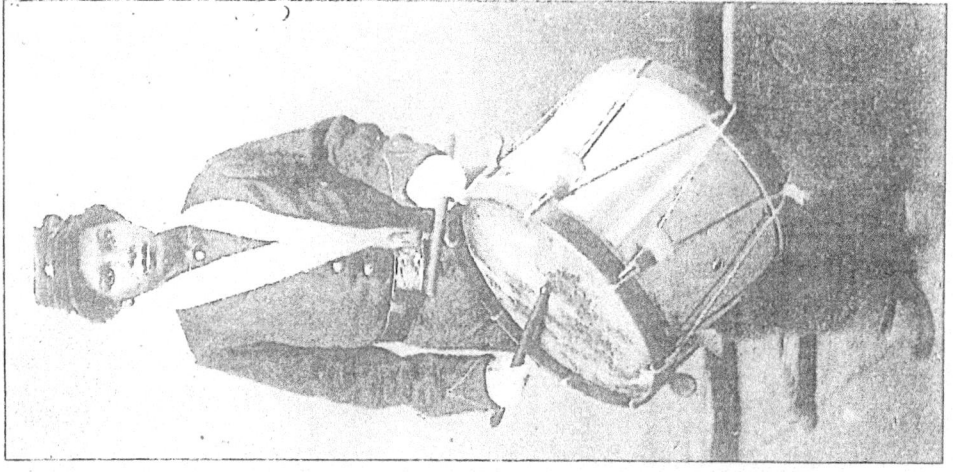

Clothed in rags, Jackson, a contraband, entered a Union camp and was uniformed as a drummer boy for the 79th United Stated Colored Troops. His photographs were circulated in northern states to inspire black men to enlist in the Union forces. An excellent reenactment role with many learning experiences can be provided for teenage boys trained to become drummer boys. *Library of Congress*

Chapter 6
Why Become a Civil War Reenactor?

One morning, or perhaps late one evening during the War Between the States, two fugitive slaves, a boy named Jackson and a man named Gordon, appeared ragged and worn seeking refuge among Union troops. Jackson became a Union drummer boy in one regiment. and Gordon became an infantry soldier in another. Each had fled from people who had not cared about their living conditions while in bondage. Neither had been clothed or fed well.

Little or nothing is known about their mothers, fathers, sisters or brothers, let alone grandparents, aunts, and uncles--but both Jackson and Gordon had had relatives just as all people do. However, the folks who had towered over them as slave masters and overseers, had made it impossible for them to live within peaceful homes and enjoy the love of their families. No records seem to exist of Jackson's family, the folks who owned him, or the place from whence he came. Only his torn, tattered clothing told the story of his past. Forced family separations and painful living conditions left reliance upon vague memories to constitute his only record of a family.

Gordon, the records show, had been whipped on Christmas day.(1,p.9) He had escaped from his master in Mississippi, trying desperately to leave his world of cruelty behind. His pursuers and their dogs tracked his trail as he fled towards Baton Rouge, Louisiana. He rubbed onions upon himself to foil the scent of yelping, barking dogs after wading through countless creeks and swamps on his long arduous journey. He ate little and slept many days in the woods before he reached the Union camp. His clothing, like those of Jackson, revealed a sad tale of unkindness. This photo of his scarred, tortured body revealed to the world his pain-filled life as a slave. (See page 94.)

Gordon's energy and intelligence were put to use as a guide for the Union troops. During one of his military ventures, he was taken prisoner by the rebels in Louisiana. He was tied up, beaten severely, and left for dead, but he escaped and returned to camp.

If by some mysterious streak of divine good fortune, some one peered into the past and identified the names of the persons who were the parents and kinfolk of Jackson and Gordon, who among the black people living today would be their descendants?

A Fugitive Who Fled for Freedom

Fig. 60. Gordon, an Infantry Soldier *Library of Congress USZ62-98515*

Historians may never record the names of Jackson's or Gordon's kinfolk, or the names of millions of others whose remains floated in rivers, and streams or who were placed in unmarked graves. However, their descendants may be alive today.

People of color, as civilian reenactors wearing clothing as worn by slaves, give honor to the family heritage of Jackson and Gordon, and thousands, no, millions like them.

The answer to the question, *Why become a civilian Civil War reenactor?* is revealed in the reason that their stories of escape exist. The Civil War service of Jackson and Gordon,[1] like thousands of other fugitive slaves in the Civil War, earned freedom for themselves, their kinfolk, and present generations.

That freedom has descended to all through countless generations. Today, people of color enjoy the freedoms for which Jackson, Gordon and thousands of others fought and died. Therein lies the real reason for people of color (African-Americans) to become civilian Civil War reenactors.

---

1. Harris, Middleton A. Morris, Levitt, Roger Furman, and Ernest Smith. The Black Book. (NY: Random House 1974) p. 9; Original photographs of Gordon appeared in *Harpers Weekly,* July 4, 1863, p.429.

"Who me? I don't want to do that."

A little ditty expresses a thoughtful metaphor:

"Some folk like gray hair, some folk do, some folk do.

Some folk like *no hair*, but that's not me or you."

In making a choice of a reenactment role:

Some folk like to wear the clothing styles of *"free people."*

<u>Most</u> folk do, most folk do.

Some folk *lack* interest in the clothing styles of *slave people*.

<u>Most</u> folk do, most folk do.

When asked to reenact in the role of a slave, one might answer,

"Who me? I don't want to do that."

Descendants of slave people may select the portrayal of slaves as a reenactment role when they realize their unique privilege to bestow deserved *honor* upon the lives of their ancestors. Reenactors in the role of slaves have the unique opportunity to reward slave ancestors with something they did not receive while in bondage, *respect* and *recognition* as human beings and for the vast contributions they made through their unpaid labor to the settlement and building of this country. In that role, reenactors inform and compel viewers to give attention to the numerous skills, musical creations, and inventive genius of those in slavery.

In that role, reenactors represent the remnants of their splintered families left on plantations when husbands and sons stole away to serve in the Union Army. They fought while steeped in hope that someday the generations that followed would be free. Reenactors make up that generation. In that role, reenactors represent the sons and husbands who died on the battlefield, many without ever having received half the pay of white soldiers or any pay for their service. They fought, not so much for money, but for the freedom of a people.

In that role, reenactors represent the hopes and dreams of a people who longed to be free to enjoy the fruits of their labor and the bond of love within their families without fear of forced separations.

Beyond all the foregoing statements, a fact remains, that in the role of a slave character at a Civil War battle reenactment, people of color honor themselves as they honor slave ancestors. Such honor is evident as shown in the following two first-person accounts of reenactment experiences. The first is written by the author and the second one is written by Ernestine Johnson.

"Who me? I don't want to do that."

Reenactment Experiences

Before delving into why I remain a reenactor after my first experience, I will begin by writing an essay about it.

It was exciting. My husband Joel and I had arrived relaxed and ready for a new adventure on Thursday evening in our motor home. It was the weekend of February 14-17, 2002 at the reenactment of the Florida Civil War Battle of Olustee located near Lake City, Florida.

Then for three mornings, we were awakened at 6:00 A.M. to the unexpected sounds of Confederate bugles and drums, and within a few short hours, we heard the sounds of thousands of feet passing in front of our tent. We witnessed the awesome sight of several regiments of Confederate soldiers in all their colorful gray regalia with rifles pointed upwards, haversacks and swords swinging by their sides. The scene was a bit frightening. Later in the day, ladies strolled by wearing an array of long bouffant dresses in a rainbow of colors held out with hooped skirts; their heads covered with veiled-feathered-flowered hats, umbrellas, gloves and purses--all casually walking along gracefully or entering sutler tents to purchase jewelry, accessories or perhaps another outfit.

My question, 'What are you dressed like?' directed to several reenactors received friendly responses like: "I'm dressed as a country gentleman," or "A Confederate" or "Union military officer" or "an undertaker."

As we browsed around in scores of sutler tents, (exact replicas of the Civil War era) we found displayed for purchase every item used during the Civil War. There were copies of the Yankee New Testament Bible, The Confederate New Testament Bible, and numerous Civil War books; in addition, every type of male and female clothing item imaginable. The sutlers sold all needs of both Union and Confederate soldiers from their boots and hats to their mess kits and fighting pieces. (Sutlers with their wares, I learned, followed the soldiers' camps during the war.)

For all three days of the event, we had the use of a tent loaned for our displays. We were given a place on the planned program to inform visitors about our theme, *The Service of Civilian People of Color in the Civil war*. As on-lookers stopped by our tent, K. O. Mitchell and Joel V. Fears, Sr. told them about the Olustee Battle and the involvement of three black units: the 54th Massachusetts Colored Regiment, the First North Carolina Colored and the Eighth United States Colored Infantry.

Visitors heard the stories that I told about the services rendered by black women in the Civil War. Three persons costumed to represent the women were: Sarah Rone as Elizabeth Keckley, Ernestine Johnson as Harriet Tubman and Sameasha Johnson as Susie King Taylor.

"Who me? I don't want to do that."

Sharing our first reenactment experience were members of the Central Florida Chapter of the African-American Historical and Genealogical Society together with students and adults from Shiloh Baptist Church, Daytona Beach, FL. Our presence was representative of the civilian population of black people during the Civil War. We were first-time reenactors dressed in slave attire and clothing worn by free people of color. Because ours was a history-making presentation, television and newspaper reporters were present to give extensive coverage to our participation. Photographs were taken of our displays: *Secret Symbols Sewn into Underground Railroad Quilts* and photographs of civilian people of color who gave service in the Civil War.

The climax of the weekend for me and all visitors, was the sight of 2500 reenactors of Confederate and Union troops in a fierce reenactment battle staged in the exact area where the Battle of Olustee took place February 20, 1864.

My first Olustee reenactment experience was personally gratifying because it gave me the opportunity to dress in the slave clothing of my ancestors and share little-known facts about African-American history with folk from places all over the country. Our presence was welcomed by the planners of the program, Eric Hague and Martha Nelson. So often we heard from visitors: "I am so happy to see you here." "Be sure to come back next year." and "Your program was very enjoyable." "I learned so much that I did not know." Those remarks made my first reenactment experience so very worthwhile and influenced my resolve to remain with the hobby."

Why I Remain a Reenactor After My First Experience

When I later purchased the book, <u>Like Men of War, Black Troops in the Civil War, 1862-1865,</u> written by Noah A. Trudeau and read accounts in the words of the black soldiers who survived that horrible 'baptism in fire' from Confederate guns on February 20, 1864 during the Olustee Battle, I wanted to continually support the three black units who fought in the battle by representing their families they had left back home. (1,pp.137-155) My decision became definite, I would become and remain a reenactor for a long, long time. Now, I proudly costume myself in the clothing of my slave ancestors, for whom thousands of brave black soldiers gave their lives in the Civil War.

In his book, Trudeau described the Olustee Battle in the letters of Lieutenants Oliver North, E. Lewis, Andrew F. Ely, and other survivors; together with newspaper accounts. He quoted the correspondent, Corporal James Henry Gooding of the 54th Massachusetts, who sent reports to the *New Bedford Mercury*. Gooding was taken prisoner and died in Andersonville Confederate Prison several months after the battle. All of the writers were on the scene and therefore qualified to give eye witness accounts of the Olustee Battle. (See Chapter 7 for details of the Olustee Battle.)

In addition to learning about the battle, I was further influenced to become a reenactor by the fact that black soldiers endured incidents of racial attacks from Union whites. They encountered difficulties on two fronts: within their ranks and from the Rebels. Yet, they fought valiantly and remained loyal soldiers.

Since I decided to remain a reenactor, in order to make sure that I, as a reenactor, could answer questions and make accurate comments about the service of people of color during the Civil War, I needed to become aware of how Negroes served, not only the Union but also in the Confederacy. Some persons may wonder as I did: how necessary is it to know how blacks served in the Confederacy? What did they do? Were they enlisted as soldiers?

I discovered that Bell Irvin Wiley, a professional historian wrote a book published in 1965 by Louisiana University titled, Southern Negroes, 1861-1865. It was well researched. (I highly recommend its reading by every Civil War reenactor.) A quote from the preface reads, "This study tells of the experience of the Negroes during the most significant period of their history in America." The reference was to the Civil War years. Two chapters discussed in detail Negroes as *Military Laborers, and Soldiers*. I noted the contents of this book as I realized the significance of the menial roles of Negroes sent from Southern plantations to Confederate camps.

Many were cooks who were more proficient than whites in that type of work. Their service was in great demand. Following an article's appearance in the *Southern Cultivator*, May-June issue, 1862, praising the work of black cooks, four Negro cooks were assigned to each Confederate company. Then "Congress passed an act authorizing payment of fifteen dollars a month and clothing to the cooks. Slaves might be employed with their masters consent." (2,p.111)

"Slaves and free Negroes were employed as hospital attendants, ambulance drivers and stretcher bearers. Their duties in hospitals were the cleaning of the wards, cooking, serving, washing and sometimes attending the patients....The compensation allowed for each colored hospital worker was four hundred dollars a year (in 1864). Clothing was furnished by the Negroes or their owners."(2, p.113) For the slaves, their masters received the cash commutation.

Negroes were employed in great numbers on railroads in the Confederacy; in the manufacture of powder and arms and as teamsters. Heavy demands were placed on blacks to repair roads and bridges and even to build new roads. They worked in the iron mines of the southern states. Many worked at Tredegar Iron Works in Richmond where Civil War cannons were built. (The 1861 gun foundry building still stands. It houses Confederate artifacts and serves as the main visitor center for Richmond National Battlefield Park. The photograph of the cannon in the front of this book was taken at the Tredegar Iron Works site.)

However, the greatest number of Negroes were used in the construction of defense works. The most laborious work involved cutting down trees, piling dirt and sand upon them to form batteries. Timber was piled in the earth as the foundation and mounds of dirt bags were piled on top forming a battery. The slaves were used to repair and build forts as the one in South Carolina named Fort Wagner. They dug canals, constructed breast works and dug trenches. They formed an army of laborers for the Confederacy.

"In the beginning of the war, slave owners quickly agreed to send their property as laborers without receiving any wages for them. They even provided the work tools and overseers to supervise them. Even though newspapers advertised that a payment of fifteen dollars a month, food and medical care would be paid to slave owners or to free Negroes who hired themselves to work as laborers," as the war progressed, the policy of hiring Negroes became more difficult as slave owners feared the loss of their property and were not sure that their physical needs were being met. (2,p.115) In addition to that, planters began to object to the hiring of free Negroes. As a result, after the first year of the war, the Confederacy had to resort to impressment of free Negroes to secure sufficient numbers of black laborers. (See Appendix D, Impressment of Negroes) There were conflicts which arose out of the impressment laws of the states relating to Negro labor and those of the Confederate government.

During the last two years of the war, as the need for more whites on the battlefields became apparent, impressment efforts were increased but the requisitioned number of slaves and free people to do the menial labor was not met. President Jefferson Davis made a proposal for the organization of "forty thousand slaves into a sort of labor corps"...and "offering freedom to those who should render loyal service to the end of the war."(2,p.121) But this measure provoked more controversy than the conflict over whether impressed slaves should work only to protect the state or for the military at large in any place. Near the close of the war, slave owners held a tighter grip on their slave property especially after the issue of the Emancipation Proclamation because they believed that the slaves would be freed if the Confederacy lost the war. It was not due to a lack of patriotism that slave owners began to hold on to their slaves and refuse to send them as laborers, the planters voiced dislike for the methods used to take their property under impressment and sometimes felt the supplying of slave labor was not done equally.

Slave owners complained: the work was injurious to the health of their slaves; they were not fed well nor given medical attention; they were punished severely; and many opportunities to escape to Union lines prevailed. Planters received money for their slaves killed near battle lines, but they felt that the payments received did not match the true value of their slave property.

The slaves did not like the hard labor required for building Confederate defenses, nor their lack of freedom for rest or relaxation which they had experienced on the plantation. They were closely watched until returning to the plantations or until they ran off to join the Yankees.

"Bell Irvin Wiley, author of Southern Negroes, 1861-1865, in Chapter IX titled *Soldiers*, stated, "During the period of the Confederacy the question of making a soldier out of the Negro received considerable attention." (2,p.146) Wiley continued throughout the chapter in great detail quoting the views and counter views of persons about the issue. Sources for documentation were cited describing intense feelings on both sides, the favoring of enlistment of Negroes and opposition. While some speakers in the Confederate Congress made proposals advocating the recruiting of slaves as a necessity, others vehemently objected for various reasons with impressive arguments. Anxiety was expressed about the effect of arming blacks to serve along side white soldiers: fear of turning their weapons towards them; questioning of Negro's willingness and ability to fight; and whether or not they should be declared free after the war. From Wiley's research, he concluded: "There seems to be no evidence that the Negro soldiers authorized by the Confederate Government ever went into battle. This gives rise to the question as to whether or not any Negroes ever fought in the Confederate ranks." (2.p.160) However, the debate still rages on and other authors express varying views. (Reenactors should not attempt to settle the debate.)

Perhaps many of the reports of Negroes fighting in the Confederate army originated from close attendance of the body servants to their masters during battles. Body servants occasionally took "pot shots at the Yankees." (2,p.161) Some body servants also wore uniforms. (See Appendix E, Marlboro Jones, Body Servant.) In response to the question, "If the rebel leaders were to arm the slaves, what would be its effect? One Negro responded to Sherman and others January 12, 1865, 'I think they would fight as long as they were before the bayonet, and just as soon as they could get away, they would desert.'(2,p.162)

---

1. Trudeau, Noah A. Like Men of War. Black Troops in the Civil War, 1862-1865. NJ: Castle Books, 2002.
    Trudeau reports eyewitness accounts of other Civil War battles in which black soldiers engaged. Readers will find great admiration for the bravery of all black units. There was and never could have been a greater sacrifice for freedom than the lives of those black men given on the Battlefield at Olustee. The Olustee Battle is described in Chapter 7 of this text, *Reenacting in Military Units*.

2. Wiley, Bell I. Southern Negroes, 1861-1865. Baton Rouge, LA: Louisiana Univ. 1965.

I'll Never Forget My First Olustee Reenactment Experience
By Ernestine Johnson

Fig. 61. Reenactor Ernestine Johnson as Harriet Tubman, meets Confederate reenactor, Douglas Jarrett at Olustee.
Courtesy Joy Dickinson

"Before detailing my first reenactment experience, I will share this: I learned a lot at Olustee. Having the opportunity to engage in *below the surface* dialogue with sentimental Confederate flag wavers proved to be very beneficial, especially my conversation with a Confederate reenactor who is married to an African-American woman. My dialogue with this gentleman helped me come face-to-face with some of my stereotypes and prejudices.

I was very curious about the people who participated in Civil War reenactments, and I wanted to really understand the mindset of the Confederate flag supporters who say the flag should be waving as a special mark in American history. My Olustee experience gave me a better understanding of both of these issues.

"As I walked into the park grounds, it became immediately obvious to me that my presence was a surprise to those in attendance on the grounds. My group was making history. This was the first reenactment at Olustee in which people of color had participated as civilian reeanactors. (Three black units fought in the Civil War Battle at Olustee so the presence of black men in Union blue in past reenactments had always been there.) My eyes met their gazes. I saw a look of curiosity in their eyes that seemed to beg the question, 'What do we have going on here?' I was dressed in a long black unadorned shift dress, old-fashioned black boots, 1800's style, a small fringed shawl draped around my neck and the ubiquitous head scarf of the black slave woman.

"Then, it became my turn to be surprised. While walking around taking in the ante-bellum atmosphere, I began to experience some unexpected tension and apprehension within. I had not given much thought about what to expect from the day. And now, I was beginning to feel like I had been transported back to the time of chattel slavery, something I had often wondered and dreamed about.

"The smoky smell of burning wood hung in the air. Later, I learned that scores of reenactors had been camping out for several days, a ritual among the reenactors. To my right, I heard the call and response barking out from a military drill officer. I slowed my steps to see what was going on. I saw about a hundred men dressed in Confederate gray marching in a military drill with a rifle upon each shoulder. I began to feel more uneasy.

"As I looked at the people walking about the grounds, I was somewhat amazed at seeing the extent of dress and paraphernalia people had gone to in recreating this era in history. It was equally amazing to see a multitude of people involved in this reenactment business, men, women and children. Some women were dressed in, what I would describe as everyday wear; simple calico fabric dresses and big white aprons, outfitted with a basket or some other type household item.

"Men in everyday wear were dressed in dark, solid color trousers, complete with suspenders, big long sleeve shirts, and wearing large brim, sun-shielding hats. Many were carrying some type of utility tool, or leading a horse, as if in the process of doing some type of farm labor.

"I noticed how others were dressed. They were very fashionable, dressed to the hilt in 1800s fancy ante-bellum styles, what I describe as "high society" clothing. This is a fashion show scene. One such family, a father, mother and their children, including a baby in an ornately decorated carriage of the period, walked in my direction. They passed by with a very quiet and dignified attitude. However, the parents appeared to be uncomfortable with my presence. It looked like they were trying to ignore me, which was hard to do considering our nearness to one another. This entire family looked like the old photographs seen of wealthy people, unsmiling from this era. The gentleman was dressed in a black top hat. The lady and her daughter were wearing long beautiful floor-length bright colored dresses with wide hoops, fancy hats and gloves. Each one carried a parasol.

"Then, an eerie scene took place. A man on a huge white horse came slowly towards me. He was wearing a big hat, *plantation master, Gone with the Wind, style*. He was checking me out with the same curiosity as the park personnel. Something was beginning to rise and stand up in me as our eyes met. I think he sensed the warrior spirit of Harriet Tubman, my character, emanating from me. He greeted me with a reserved, 'Good Morning,' I returned the greeting. A reporter joined me as I continued my tour. She was gathering information to report on the day's event for a newspaper.

"I saw hundreds of, what I later learned were called, *sutler tents,* in which merchants were selling all kinds of 1800s reproductions and replicas of Civil War paraphernalia: fabric, clothing, tools, household wares, guns, Confederate and Union uniforms, flags, books, foods and whatever else, common to the Civil War era.

"Finally, members of my African-American reenactment group arrived. They were members of the Central Florida Chapter, Afro-American Historical and Genealogical Society. We spent the day presenting information about the contributions of African-American women in the Civil War, namely the stories of Elizabeth Keckley, Charlotte Forten, Susie King Taylor and my number one heroine, Harriet Tubman. In addition, we presented discussions about secret symbols sewn into quilts used on the "Underground Railroad" to give messages of direction to slaves planning to escape to free states in the North.

"We became increasingly aware that our appearance and performance were the firsts in the Olustee reenactment experience. Throughout the two days at Olustee, we made friends with reenactors and visitors. We met some of the African-American reenactors of the famed 54th Massachusetts Infantry, United States Colored Troops, made famous by the movie *Glory* which starred Denzel Washington. I found the troops' presence very comforting.

"We received a lot of well wishes and pleasantries for our participation. Received were many invitations to participate in other Civil War reenactments along with numerous requests for presentations at schools and churches. The people who stopped at our display, reenactors and park visitors, opened their hearts and shared old family stories about their loss of ancestors' land, and other family wealth as a result of the Civil War. Some people shared historical information about safe houses and "Underground Railroad" stations rediscovered in their hometowns in Northern states. We heard about fascinating family secrets and other discoveries that people learned through family genealogy research. There were a lot of exchanges about quilts and quilting.

"Most surprising, was the intimacy of feelings people expressed when broaching sensitive discussions about race relations in America. Many people seemed to have a need to talk. Some spoke of confusion and a loss at not having the opportunity to speak openly with African-Americans about the subject of race. I was dumbfounded when some complained about the lack of interest by African-Americans in Civil War history and reenactment.

"I noticed that only a few people appeared disturbed by our attendance as they silently poked through our display area with a scowl on their faces. We saw very few African-Americans among the reported 5,000 plus people at Olustee. Besides the people from my reenactment group,

My First Olustee Reenactment Experience

I recall one African-American woman, who appeared to be married to one of the tent merchants. There were a few African-American kids among the 1,100 visiting boy scouts. Included with this group was one uncomfortable-in-appearance looking African-American dad. I observed him looking fervently at the ante-bellum scenes around him with no signs of pleasant thoughts upon his face. He did not converse with any of us at our tent.

"At the end, I was very pleased and excited about my Olustee experience. I've participated in a second Olustee event and several small Civil War reenactments since first reenacting at Olustee. Often, I am the only African-American person at an event. I participate as Mrs. Harriet Tubman and I take great pride in presenting her story and the contributions of African-American people in the atmosphere of Civil War reenactments. I go dressed in 1860s style clothing of the Civil War era, carry books and other paraphernalia to document the stories I tell of African-American people during this period in America's history.

"Participating in Civil War reenactments, and having dialogue with the descendants of former slave holders in *our* voice, telling *our* African-American story from *our* perspective, is vitally necessary for everyone."

What's It About, "Military Reenacting," At Civil War Reenactments

Fig. 63. NICHOLAS BIDDLE
Courtesy, Alex Chamberlain Collection, USAMHI

Biddle shares a history with Crispus Attucks. Both were former slaves and the first to shed blood in two of America's wars, the Revolutionary War and the Civil War.

Chapter 7
Reenacting in Military Units

The extent of loyal, sacrificial service given by former slaves and "free men of color" in military service during the Civil War is of primary interest to Civil War reenactors. Some facts may be barely known as the story of Nicholas Biddle, a runaway slave, who, like Crispus Attucks, shared a common history. Attucks, a black escaped slave, was the first to die in the American Revolutionary War during the "Boston Massacre" of 1770. Biddle, an eager sixty-five year old former slave met with disaster when he insisted on going to war in a *non-enlisted* capacity immediately following Lincoln's call for troops in the War Between the States.

Two days following Lincoln's call, Biddle left his means of livelihood, "selling ice cream and oysters in Pottsville, Pennsylvania," to attach himself to the Washington Artillerists. When the Artillerists left Baltimore and paraded towards the train depot enroute to Washington, they were eager to offer protection for the Nation's Capitol. Biddle, in military uniform marching with the troops, drew the pleasure and delight of people in the black population along the parade route, but his presence was particularly a source of annoyance to agitators who voiced hatred to see a "Nigger in uniform"[1,pp.25] An object hurled by one bystander struck Biddle in the face slicing it to the bone. Although the troops arrived in Washington, D.C. and were received with acclamation, Biddle dropped from sight. In later years, friends engraved upon his tombstone:

> "His has the distinction of shedding the first blood in the late war for the Union, being wounded while marching through Baltimore with the first volunteers from Schuylkill County, 18 April, 1861."[1,pp.25-26]

Upon first hearing rumors and rumblings of war, like Nicholas Biddle, black men rushed to give service and just as quickly, were turned away. Without hesitation, runaway slaves were hastily returned to their masters.

Even without expressed orders, uniforms or weapons, free blacks who were former slaves, organized militia units and held marching drills--only to be disbanded. No troops could be organized without President Lincoln's orders. Widespread opposition to black enlistment blocked every effort of black men to serve in the military. Foremost was Lincoln's *hands-off* policy regarding the use of escaped slaves. The president wanted to keep the loyalty of the slave-holding states: Kentucky, Missouri, Maryland and Delaware. Coupled with the President's efforts to refrain from doing anything to abolish slavery or to cause those border states to secede, was the

Military Units

strong feeling of whites who did not want to fight beside black men. Nevertheless, the efforts of black men, determined in their resolve to fight, were fueled with the belief, eloquently expressed by Frederick Douglass, that black men would prove their manhood and the war would put an end to slavery. Other abolitionists loudly urged black men to enlist. Gradually, Congress passed legislation aimed at abolishing slavery and the resistance to enlisting blacks in the military.

In September 1862, five months after the bombardment of Fort Sumter on April 12, 1861, Lincoln issued a preliminary emancipation which opened the door to black enlistment. Two months later, Lincoln authorized organization of the first black regiment. Hundreds of freed slaves on the South Carolina coast became the 1st South Carolina Volunteers under the leadership of Colonel Thomas Wentworth Higginson. Higginson kept a journal and published his experiences in <u>Army Life in a Black Regiment.</u> (N.Y.: Norton, 1984) with detailed descriptions of his soldiers' courage and willingness to fight. He recorded the words of songs and "escape-from slavery experiences" that they shared with each other as they sat around campfires in the evening.

More importantly, the men in every military encounter proved their fitness to make good soldiers, thereby physically discrediting the opinions of white officers and soldiers who held strong negative feelings about black men and their ability to fight. Even after hearing loud cries from Confederates declaring that "black soldiers captured in battle would be enslaved and not treated as prisoners of war," did not deter the onslaught of black men by the thousands from joining Union ranks. Thousands chose to join the fighting forces in the Union navy. Whenever possible, escaped slaves boarded Union gunboats.

When the Emancipation Proclamation became law on January 1, 1863, all barriers were shattered, and black men enlisted like a monumental black tidal wave rushing towards shore. Historic accounts of skirmishes and battles where black units fought carried countless stories of heroism noting how they fought and died for the Union cause and the liberty of an enslaved people.

Equally as important as the wearing of the reenactor's Civil War uniform and the training to fire weapons safely is the reading of a collection of books with well-documented accounts of black involvement in the Civil War. No better source of documentation exists than recorded eye-witness accounts of soldiers who survived the battles. With this background knowledge, reenactors can truly experience the heat of battle. For a reenactor to add the personal depth of meaning to his role, he needs knowledge of the historic facts involved in the background of each battle in which he participates: the *who* involved, the *why,* the *what*, the *when* and the *where* it happened. Of no less importance is the *how* the battle was fought and won, and by whom.

A perfect example to stress this point is to read the account in the words of the black soldiers who survived a horrible "baptism in fire" from Confederate guns on February 20, 1864 during the Florida Civil War Battle of Olustee. Even reenactors in the roles of civilians will take to their hearts the soul stirring details of that battle and feel compelled to support the deeds of the three black units who fought at Olustee. Civilian reenactors may proudly represent the soldiers' families left at home, both those fortunate enough to be free, and others left behind under the heavy yoke of bondage.

In his book, <u>Like Men of War, Black Troops in the Civil War, 1862-1865,</u> Noah A. Trudeau[2] described the Olustee Battle in the written records of survivors; together with news articles from the New York Times, Philadelphia Press and other newspapers. Each writer's document gave descriptive accounts of the encounter between Federal and Rebel troops. Their recorded memories are quoted by Trudeau in the sequence of how the Olustee Battle took place.

Three black units fought in the Battle of Olustee: the 8th Regiment United States Colored Troops, the North Carolina First Regiment Colored Volunteers and the 54th Massachusetts Infantry Colored Volunteers.

At dawn the morning of February 20, 1864 when Federal troops set out from the town of Barbers east of Jacksonville, Florida, marching with unloaded weapons enroute to Lake City to "destroy a railroad," the main supply route for sending beef to Confederate troops in Georgia, no one envisioned a fierce battle in the afternoon with Rebel forces, which ended in the loss of hundreds of lives.

Unaware of Georgia reinforcements to the area, mild skirmishes with Confederate pickets a few days before left Union officers unaware of Rebel preparations for battle lurking ahead. "Shoot and run tactics" drew Union leading troops: the 7th Connecticut, the 7th New Hampshire and the 8th United States Colored Troops directly into Rebel lines of fire.

At the beginning of the encounter with the Rebels, Lt. Oliver North of the 8th United States Colored Troops stated, "I was within earshot when I heard the order of General Seymour, "Put your regiment in Colonel Fribley."(2, p.142) Colonel Charles Fribley, commander of the 8th United States Colored Troops, was mortally wounded within twenty minutes of the firing. That group of brave soldiers, the 8th USCT, without its leader, instantly came within a few feet face to face with the Rebels. (USCT is the acronym for United States Colored Troops.) Only half of them had muskets and those who had muskets had not been adequately trained to load and fire them.

So the men in the 8th USCT "cowered like frightened sheep" as bullets ripped through their bodies and they began "falling like leaves in autumn"...."The loss of their commander had disordered the regiment, but they did not scatter as the 7th New Hampshire." After ninety minutes of the most intensive, destructive fire, the few men who survived stumbled to the rear.(2, p.143)

Further details of the Olustee Battle in Trudeau's book, Like Men of War, described the scene that followed the fighting. When the shooting stopped and the Union soldiers and calvary retreated, as black men lay wounded in the blood-soaked field, their mangled bodies groaning in pain, Confederate soldiers strolled among them shooting "their brains out."(2,p.151) Those wounded men in Union blue died on the battlefield where a slight chance of survival may have been extended had they been taken as "prisoners of war."

Dr. A. P. Heichold, the surgeon of the 8th USCT, who, early in the battle had foreseen the inevitable end as favoring the Rebels, attempted to load as many of the wounded as possible on wagons for the retreat back to Barbers, a small town East of Jacksonville. Many wounded were piled into a train car located on the nearby train tracks. However, because of a broken flue, the locomotive would not move.

The able-bodied men in the 54th Massachusetts tied ropes around their waists and with their manly strength pulled the train down the tracks until they reached Finegan's Camp, where horses were attached to finish the task.(2, p.152) The Union forces lost the battle.

Casualties in the 8th USCT were extremely high because this unit was among the leading regiments as the Union forces left Barbers walking towards Lake City about 6:30 A.M. on the morning of the battle.

The 8th USCT faced the enemy during the first phase of the battle. After the 7th Connecticut, the 7th New Hampshire and several New York Units had begun retreating to the rear, the other two black units: the North Carolina 1st and the 54th Massachusetts, were ordered up front to face the Rebels. They were ordered in near the end of the battle in an effort to "save the Union troops from complete annihilation."(2,p.148) A small contingent of the 7th Connecticut returned to the front in battle lines with the two black units.

Before advancing towards Lake City, Union commander General Truman Seymour had not sent scouts to pinpoint the position of the Confederates. He was unaware of the Georgia troops that had been sent to the area to bolster the 1,200 Rebels under General Joseph Finegan's command when the Union boats docked in Jacksonville on February 7. There was no expectation of meeting the Confederates prior to their arrival in Lake City. So they were taken by surprise as they advanced with unloaded muskets and artillery. As a result, the Battle of Olustee resulted in a defeat for the Union.

Fig. 64. REENACTOR MEL TURNER
Olustee Reenactment, February 15, 2003

The knowledge of what happened at the Florida Civil War Battle and at other battles in which black troops fought creates an effective stimulant for prospective military and civilian reenactors. Each battle which involved black troops is described in Trudeau's book.

The story of the Battle at Olustee provides for America, great admiration for the patriotism, courage and bravery of not only those three black units at Olustee, but all who served in the Union Army and Union Navy during the Civil War. There never could have been a greater sacrifice for freedom than the lives of those black men in the 8th United States Colored Troops given on the Battlefield at Olustee on February 20, 1864. A reenactment of the battle is held each February at the Olustee Battlefield Historic State Park.[3] Thousands of reenactors come to participate.

Reenactors will find reading Emilio's book, A Brave Black Regiment, The History of the 54th Massachusetts, 1863-1865 (NY: De Capo Press, 1995) most inspiring to read.

As Civil War reenactors, both as civilians and soldiers in the military, an honor is bestowed upon each individual, whether wearing the Union blue, the drab clothing of slaves or the better dressed garments of the fortunate few "free people of color."

1. Quarles, Benjamin. The Negro In The Civil War. Boston: Little, Brown and Co., 1969.

2. Trudeau, Noah Andre. Like Men of War, Black Troops in the Civil war, 1862-1865. NY: Little, Brown, Inc., 2002.

3. The park is located twenty miles east of I-75 and Lake City, FL, and fifty miles west of I-95 and Jacksonville, FL.
Mailing address: Olustee Battlefield Historic State Park, P.O. Drawer G, White Springs, FL 32096 Tel. (386)397 2733
Announcements of upcoming dates for all Civil War Battle Reenactments are placed on the internet and in Civil War publications, like the *Camp Chase Gazette*, a monthly magazine. e-mail www.campchase.com

Fig. 65. Reenactors: KARL KING   LEON VAUGHN   JOHN PEDEN
54th Massachusetts Volunteer Infantry Co. B

AT REST
Fig. 66. THE 54th MASSACHUSETTS VOLUNTEER INFANTRY

Meet Civil War Reenactors

Civil War reenactors proudly represent the famed 54th Massachusetts Infantry (Colored) Regiment. It was the first regiment organized in the North or free states following Lincoln's Emancipation Proclamation. Governor John A. Andrews of Massachusetts led the enlistment effort and sought officers as commanders who had military experience and faith in the ability of black men to render military service. Greatly influenced by Frederick Douglass, black men from other states joined in the ranks of the 54th. This regiment, featured in the movie *Glory,* turned the tide of public opinion earning much deserved recognition for their bravery in the assault on Fort Wagner July 18, 1863.

The young soldier selected by Governor Andrews to lead those valiant troops into battle was Colonel Robert Shaw, who lost his life in the fight at Fort Wagner and was buried in a trench with his fallen heroes. Colonel Shaw was held in the highest esteem by his men and by all who knew him. Charlotte Forten, a free black teacher from Philadelphia who had come to teach the children of former slaves on nearby St. Helena Island in South Carolina, met Colonel Shaw and recorded in her diary after she learned of his death, "I recall him as a much loved friend. Yet I saw him but a few times...Oh, it is terrible. It seems very, very hard to me that the best and noblest must be the earliest called away. Especially has it been throughout this dreadful war." (1, p.92)

Noah Andre Trudeau, in Like Men of War, Black Troops in the Civil War 1862-1865, described with illustrations and in great detail the battle at Fort Wagner. Civil War reenactors who learn from survivors' quotes from the battle at Fort Wagner will feel that those soldiers proved to the President and to the country what the soldiers already knew, that they were "men" capable of stalwart military service. Knowledge of how those brave men in the 54th, while receiving no pay for more than a year, went into battle facing an onslaught of cannon shells and musketry, suffered and died in the Union's tragic loss at Fort Wagner, greatly bolsters the resolve of reenactors to honor their service in the Civil War. The courageous fighters in the 54th, and blacks in every Civil War regiment, conscious of their dignity as soldiers, demanded to be recognized as soldiers.

Reenacting as a part of the 54th Massachusetts Infantry, as well as all of the other black units that fought in the Civil War, enables men to experience the triumphant spirit of those thousands of fighters who paid for freedom with the currency of their lives. Three reenactors: Mel Reid, Clifford Pierce, and John Peden proudly wear the Union blue in Civil War Battle reenactments in which the 54th fought. Their views about the hobby follow.

---

1. Burchard, Peter. Charlotte Forten, A Black Teacher in the Civil War. NY: Crown Publishers, 1995.

Fig. 67. PVT. MEL REID
54th Massachusetts Volunteer Infantry, Co. B

Mel Reid

"...those special heroes of the past are truly worthy of our
recognition as well as our responsibility to pass it on." Mel Reid

Civil War reenactor, Pvt. Mel Reid, of the 54th Massachusetts Volunteer Infantry Regiment, Company B, submitted the following about his life experiences as a reenactor.

"Growing up as a youngster, I so often wondered, but so seldom heard much about the African American experience in the American Civil War. Throughout grade school, college and beyond, it seemed as though the only roles that African Americans played were unconcerned bystanders, who were convinced and thus content, that the Civil War was indeed reserved for white men only. And perhaps worse, African Americans further appeared to have no real stake, claim or business trying to interfere with America's political and military matters such as the War Between the States, preservation of the Union, States Rights, secession and other noted issues of the time. And of course, nothing could be further from the truth. In fact, most African Americans have always seemed to understand that historically the war was about slavery and most importantly, the overall abolition of that painful piece of the past which was sometimes referred to as 'the peculiar institution.' As such, much would be gained by arming "men of color" as opposed to overlooking and/or ignoring those with so much to lose.

"The arming of men of color became an actual reality for me one evening in 1989, while attending an 1863 Abolition Rally reenactment at the Frederick Douglas Historic Site in Washington, D.C. During that particular gathering, African American men were being tactfully recruited to portray Union Soldiers in the Hollywood production of a soon to be released movie titled, GLORY. With little persuasion, I enlisted that very evening and thus, my life became richly enhanced as one of the first ever modern-day African American Civil War reenactors.

"Having proudly served in this new-found hobby for the past fourteen years has proven to be so much more than ever anticipated. In fact,

I have gained a real appreciation for historical accuracy with a specific focus and interest in that period of time between 1861 & 1865. In particular, I have learned as well as practiced various aspects of Civil War military procedures such as the proper wearing and presentation of period uniforms; battlefield tactics and strategies; rank, file and precision drilling demonstrations; and other related matters associated with life as a soldier. I have also gained a real respect for safety in that the weapons used by most Civil War reenactors are indeed real and must be treated as such. Therefore, during the actual locking-loading and firing of muskets, pistols, cannon, and other items of destruction, discretion must be the better part of valor, even in the absence of real ordinance (ammunition).

"In Addition to the aforementioned, reenacting has also afforded me the wonderful opportunity to travel to many far and distant places. Whether marching in parades through the streets of Boston, Washington, Charleston, Atlanta, St. Louis, Lake City, and countless other cities; or visiting the hallowed ground of a pristine battlefield or a majestic monument or memorial; or, perhaps making an appearance at a local school, organization or a radio and/or television show; the wealth of experience as well as emotions felt while performing these types of fun-related activities have consistently been quite moving, fulfilling, exhilarating, stimulating, motivating, and, at times, even a bit challenging.

A Challenge.

"Perhaps most importantly, those of us who proudly serve as African American Civil War reenactors fully understand also that our involvement in most activities goes far beyond normal expectations often experienced at typical reenactment gatherings. Because we are generally new and few as an overall group of less than 100 active men throughout America, we are still making our mark and/or presence known throughout the reenactment community and beyond. As such, we are also occasionally viewed as a novelty or in some instances, even as suspect. And all this, in light and in spite of the fact that the movie GLORY was released some ten-plus years ago. But, we are easily driven in our mission and purpose primarily because our very necessary piece of Civil War history has essentially been ignored or overlooked for some 130+ years. And its now up to us to tell those untold stories. This is basically why I proudly serve as a reenactor.

"And, this is why I challenge any and all African-Americans (men and women) with even the slightest interest in history culture, genealogy, ethnography, and the like to seriously consider the remarkable *world of reenacting*. After all, if we do not tell our story, then who will?

"I further offer that those who have an interest should attend a reenactment and specifically, a Civil War reenactment. There are usually several events scheduled almost every weekend throughout various parts of America. A check and/or contact with news publications or the media, bookstores, libraries, searching the web or inquiries with parks or historical organizations will very likely prove successful.

"Once one has observed and feels the further urge to become a part of it all, simply ask anyone at a reenactment how to become involved. Most individuals at reenactments are usually eager to share what they have and know. For additional information about the African American experience in the Civil War, you are further encouraged to log on to this e-mail address: http://www.54thmass.org

"Again, it is hoped that serious consideration will be given to becoming a part of the unique *brother and sisterhood of reenacting*. Be reminded too that we, as African Americans, are quite blessed and indeed fortunate to be able to stand on the shoulders of those who went before us. Given all this, it would certainly seem that the exceptional contributions of those special heroes of the past are truly worthy of our recognition as well as our responsibility to pass it on."

MILITARY REENACTORS

CHAPLAIN CLIFFORD PIERCE

PVT. JOHN PEDEN
54th Massachusetts Volunteer Infantry, Co. F.

Clifford Pierce

Chaplain Clifford Pierce "had in mind protesting" when he first attended a meeting of a Unit of the 54th. But his interest reached its peak while he was there and he was "hooked" on reenacting from that point on. That was fourteen years ago. Once Pierce learned about the names of five infantry men in the 54th who became officers while enroute to Jacksonville following the battle at Fort Wagner, he decided to reenact the role of Chaplain Samuel Harrison. Harrison was the first Chaplain of the 54th Massachusetts Infantry.

In Chaplain Pierce's words, he "gets a great feeling teaching people about history as well as having fun reenacting." He feels strongly that "as people learn more about the hobby and history of the Civil War period, they will be drawn into the hobby. "Benefits are many," he says: "camaraderie and close friendship ties; knowing and having people care about you and your family's daily lives; why it's like becoming a part of a family; when you meet, it's like a family reunion. Others can join by getting information through the media at web sites and by word-of-mouth. I've helped many people get involved with the hobby."

John Peden

John Peden's interest in the history of the area in which he learned that his wife of more than twenty-seven years was born, influenced him to consider reenacting as a hobby. She was born and raised in Sanderson, Florida in Baker County, the same neck-of-the woods in which the Civil War Battle of Olustee took place February 20, 1864. Peden became aware of the yearly reenactments at Olustee, only twelve miles from their home. He noticed that the events were not visited by "people of color" from the very area where the battle was staged but others from as far away as New York came.

John Peden, known as Elder Peden in his community, visited one of the reenactments and became the first Baker County black reenactor to proudly wear full dress Civil War garb. In his words, he claims, "I took a full launch as a pioneer, and my goal now is to bring knowledge of the history of African-American people to the very community that has been deprived of its own county history either by choice or default. I strongly recommend that anyone interested in becoming a part of the 54th Massachusetts send e-mail to chief404@aol.com to learn how to get involved here in Florida or elsewhere,"

FEMALE CONTRABANDS IN UNION SERVICE

Fig. 70. Reenactor Barbara Brockington in the role of a female conband giving service to the Union Army.
Seated left to right, Union Soldier Reenactors: Brian Bliss, Eugene Sereg and Dwight Dovel.

Fig. 71. Reenactor Pinkie Caldwell portraying the role of a female contraband. Fugitive slaves became known as "contrabands" of the Union Army when they escaped into Union lines. Once they were under the protection of the soldiers, they were considered "free." Many women served as cooks and washerwomen in camps. During the Civil War, thousands of slaves fled into Union lines to obtain freedom from bondage.

So You Want To Get Involved In Civil War Military Reenacting, How To Begin

Any African American male who becomes a reenactor to represent those fugitive slave fighters and "free men of color" who fought in the Civil War for the cause of freedom, receives from himself an honorary "Medallion of Pride" for a lifetime.

Civil War reenacting is a hobby, a fun hobby. Thousands are involved in it. The foremost requirements are sincere interest in educating the public and the desire to be as authentic in uniform and action as possible. Experienced "old timers" welcome recruits. Attendance at one Civil War reenactment to meet and talk with reenactors provides an excellent introduction to the hobby.

Invitations to become Civil War reenactors remain open for African American males to join, not only the units of the 54th Massachusetts Infantry Regiment, but *all* units of black regiments that served in the Civil War. Organized units are present in several states, If travel is necessary to reach one, the benefits of camaraderie make each trip worthwhile.

The first step is to follow the loud cries of newspaper boys from a bygone era who yelled on city streets, "READ ALL ABOUT IT!" But today, extend their familiar slogan by adding: "ON THE INTERNET, IN CIVIL WAR BOOKS, IN MAGAZINES, IN NEWSPAPERS AND IN OTHER PUBLICATIONS!"

Information on the internet lists web sites, names, addresses and telephone numbers of contacts for a number of organized African-American reenactment units. All that a prospective reenactor, or new recruit, needs to know about Civil War period requirements: the uniforms, tents, equipment, weapons and other accouterments. are readily available when contacts are made with an organized reenactment unit.

Interested persons may log on to www.Google.com or some other search engine and type in **African American Civil War Reenactment Units.** A world of information for all persons with interest in the reenactment hobby is available on the internet.

For an introduction to many topics about the Civil War and African American involvement; and a list of reenactment units with links to individual web sites, type in the following: **http://www.coax.Net/people/lwf/data.htm**

It is impossible to measure the educational value and importance of becoming "living historians" as Civil War reenactors. The sharing of historic facts along with a display of authentic impressions of specific black military men in the Civil War provide a special kind of personal joy. Reenacting affords many opportunities to present the valuable contributions made by black Americans during the Civil War. (See the Appendix A for a list of web sites with contact information to African-American Reenactment Units.)

Bibliography
Civil War Military Reenacting

Guides for Reenacting in Civil War Battle Reenactments   Titles marked with a (*) are of special help for reenactors.

Hadden, R. Lee. <u>Reliving the Civil War, A Reenactor's Handbook.</u>* Mechanicsburg, PA: Stackpole Bks., 1996.
   Hadden details everything one needs to know to begin Civil War reenacting and participating in other "living history" events. See his comprehensive bibliography for additional titles most useful for reenacting. Chapter titles include: "Civil War Uniforms," "Arms and Weapons," "Camp Life," and "Civilian Reenacting."

The Civil War

*The titles marked (++) describe the battles in which the **USCT (United States Colored Troops)** fought during the Civil War.*

Emilio, Luis. <u>A Brave Black Regiment, The History of the 54th Massachusetts, 1863-1865.</u>++ NY: De Capo Press, 1995.

Gladstone, William A. <u>Men of Color.</u>++ Gettysburg, PA: Thomas Publications, 1993.
   Gladstone includes numerous photographs of black servicemen and civilians. He gives a complete history of blacks in the Union forces. The book has photographs of people in the clothing worn during the Civil War era.

Glatthaar, Joseph. <u>The Civil War's Black Soldiers.</u>*++ National Parks Civil War Series. Eastern National Park and Monument Assn. 1996.

Higginson, Thomas Wentworth.   <u>Army Life in a Black Regiment.</u>*++ N.Y.: Norton, 1984.
   Colonel Higginson's account of his experiences as the commander of the first American regular army regiment of freed slaves. This book is a "must read" for every Civil war reenactor." In the Mid-1860s it was widely understood that black soldiers in great numbers contributed mightily to the victory of the Union side in the Civil War." Quoted from the book's preface.

Levine, Bruce. <u>Half Slave and Half Free, The Roots of Civil War.</u> NY: Hill and Wang, 1992.
   This title gives an overview of the causes of the Civil War. "Levine puts the focus where it belongs: "on slavery and the struggle to preserve or abolish it." Quote of Peter Kolchin printed on the book's cover.

Miller, William J. and Brian C. Pohanks. <u>An Illustrated History of the Civil War.</u> ++ Alexandria, VA: Time-Life Books, 2000.
   This book includes a splendid array of photographs and essays written by historians including a chapter on the 54th Massachusetts Regiment and a brief history of the participation of black troops in the Civil War.

Nalty, Bernard C. Strength for the Fight, A History of Black Americans in the
Military.++NY: The Free Press, 1986.
Two chapter titles: "Service in Time of Slavery," and "Civil War and Emancipation"

The Civil War

Nulty, William H. Confederate Florida, The Road to Olustee. ++
A detailed description of the Florida Civil War Battle of Olustee in which three U.S. Colored Troops fought: the Eighth US Colored Troops, First North Carolina Colored and the Fifty-Fourth Massachusetts Colored Regiment.

Quarles, Benjamin. Tne Negro In The Civil War.* Boston: Little, Brown and Co., 1969.

Taylor, Susie King. Reminiscences of my Life, A Black Woman's Civil War Memoirs. NY: Markus Wiener Publishing, 1988.
This autobiography covers the author's service experiences in the Civil War.

Trudeau, Noah Andre. Like Men of War, Black Troops in the Civil war, 1862-1865.++
NY: Little, Brown, Inc., 2002.
The author quotes eyewitness accounts of news reporters who were on the scene of battles and directly from the men who survived. For a true documented account of black involvement in the Civil War, this book is recommended reading.

Tucker, Phillip Thomas. From Auction Block to Glory, The African American Experience, Civil War Chronicles.++ NY: Friedman/Fairfax Publishers, 1998.
Excellent for reenactors' and students' understanding of the Civil War.

Wiley, Bell Irvin. Southern Negroes, 1861 - 1865. Baton Rouge: Louisiana State University Press, 1938.
This study is a most important one as it is one of the earliest published treatises documenting the history of Negroes during the most significant period of their history in America, the Civil War. The book's contents have strong appeal for reenactors who desire to know facts about black soldiers and their relationship to the Confederacy. Documents in the book address the controversy over whether blacks served in the Confederate army. Chapter titles include: "Body Servants," "Soldiers," and "Fighting for Freedom."

Military Prison

Burnett, William G. The Prison Camp at Andersonville, Civil War Series. National Park Civil War Service. Eastern National, 1995.

What Is Remembered

Fig. 73. REENACTOR MARY FEARS
Battle for Lake Helen at Bishop's Farm Reenactment
March 28-30, 2003

Chapter 8
Reminiscences of a Civil War Reenactment
By Mary L. Jackson Fears
The Battle for Lake Helen at Bishop's Farm
March 28-30, 2003 in Lake Helen, FL

What a week it had been! I had five sessions of storytelling at three schools between Tuesday and Thursday. They were followed with an evening of preparation for my reenactment on Friday, March 28, 2003. The reenactment site was a 45-minute drive from my Daytona Beach, Florida home. "My goodness, this gas tank is about on empty," observed my husband as we traveled by car towards Lake Helen, the battlefield site. I was dressed in my Civil War reenactment outfit, a replica of a dress which may have been worn as a slave house servant or a "free person of color" in the 1860s. I was eagerly looking forward to my third reenactment experience.

This was my first participation at "The Battle for Lake Helen at Bishop's Farm Civil War Reenactment." We arrived a little past nine and were happy to hear, "The students would not arrive until 10:00 A.M."

"Good, I have enough time to set up my displays." The informant pointed to a tent fly, not a wall tent as I had used at the Reenactment of the Battle of Olustee. But that was all right. It did not look like rain. The Florida sky was a clear blue with no clouds in sight, although it had rained cats and dogs the night before.

The young stranger approached and explained to me, "You're at station Number 8. The students will begin over the hill at the first station, then change to move to each station when they hear the sound of the cannon. You're Number 8 and when they leave you, they will go to Number 9, that's over there where all of the sutler tents are. You're the last station before they go to visit the sutlers."

The *last* station? This is my *first* time participating at this reenactment, and I am the "last" station." I am thinking, "Why are we placed last?" My thoughts raced on, "We were an important part of this thing. Why according to the few sentences printed in my high school 1940s history book about slavery, "this war was fought over the issue of slavery." I remembered that because that was about *all* that my history book stated.

My curiosity about slavery had been aroused and I went home and asked my grandma if her mother had been a slave. She said, "No, she was born one year after slavery." That was all that I learned about the "issue of slavery" at that time.

We did not have a school library. My folks had not been taught about slavery either, so they did not know anything to tell me. My home town did not have a public library, but then if it had, as a black child during the days of segregation, I doubt if I could have used it.

My thoughts about being last were pushed aside, and I hurriedly arranged my demonstration. "I am here to discuss the role of *People of Color in the Civil War* with emphasis on the role of women," I would say to the students. The students would see photographs and hear the stories of Elizabeth Keckley, Susie King Taylor and Harriet Tubman--all born as slaves.

My husband would not be present. He would have talked to the students about the black men, many former slaves, who fought and died in the Civil War while receiving half the pay as white soldiers.

The students would learn that Elizabeth Keckley was extremely skilled as a seamstress. She purchased her freedom using her sewing skills and eventually became a seamstress for Mary Todd Lincoln. Madame Elizabeth, as President Lincoln addressed Mrs. Keckley, also made dresses for the wives of the congressmen. She even made dresses for Jefferson Davis' wife before she met Mrs. Lincoln.

The students would see displayed a book written by Susie King Taylor, a former slave, who became a nurse during the Civil War and would be told that she tended to the wounded from the Battle at Fort Wagner and that she followed the men in the South Carolina First Volunteers, all former slaves, from camp to camp. The students would learn how Susie King Taylor as a slave girl learned to read and write and taught the men during their hours away from duty. The students would learn about the Civil War experiences of Harriet Tubman, how she served during the Civil War as a spy, scout, and nurse and how she guided raids into Confederate territory.

They would hear the story about Charlotte Forten, a free black born in Philadelphia who became a teacher of the former slave children on St. Helena Island after the Federals had reclaimed the Sea Islands along the coast of South Carolina--all during the Civil War.

Why, I had a lot to tell and I wanted to have time for the students to ask questions. Then in addition to all of the above, I wanted to explain all about the secret codes sewn into "Underground Railroad" quilts. So over to the *information people* I packed myself, "Fifteen minutes is not enough time," I complained.

"The students have to move when the cannon goes off so they can get back to school on time."

"Well, there's a problem with that. I can't tell the difference between the cannon firing and a musket or gun firing."

"The guide with each group is supposed to tell you."

Well, I cut out a part of my planned presentation and labored to remain within the time frame as I continued to speak to the two thousand students divided into groups over a two-hour period. Yes, two thousand kids, tramped by my station for my 15-20 minute presentation! Whew!

Just as I was beginning to rest my beginning-to-get-hoarse voice, up walked a visitor and said to me, "You know, hundreds of slaves fought for the Confederacy."

I gazed at the fellow and asked, "Now, will you tell me why at every reenactment, someone comes up to tell me that?"

His response, "Well, because there is so much controversy about it."

And I'm thinking, "Now, I am not interested in fighting this war all over again, from what I have read, slaves accompanied their slave masters as *body servants;* forced to obey, they went with their slave masters to do their bidding, no matter what or where. How foolish it would have been for slaves to fight to keep themselves in bondage." I knew that slaves assisted the Confederacy in non-combat roles. They had no choice but to obey the masters for whom they served.

Then the gentlemen added, "Thousands of *free* blacks in the South fought for the Confederacy."

"Free blacks?" I said, as he walked away, "I don't believe it. I've done lots of research and I never saw anything like that."

I wished that I had had with me a copy of the letter from J. H. Stringfellow dated in February, 1865, addressed to Confederate President Jefferson Davis in which the writer stated that the "Yankees had 200,000 of our ex-slaves and we have not one soldier from that source in our ranks." (see Appendix D) Perhaps in the future, I can avoid discussions by simply giving a copy of the letter. The letter is a part of the government's Compilation of the Official Records of the Union and Confederate Armies available on the internet.

Seemingly, I had not read enough. By the way, I wondered, "Who won the Civil War Battle fought for Lake Helen at Bishop's Farm? Saturday, the public comes. I would return that next day as a reenactor. I needed to find that out.

What made the entire experience more than a pleasure was the one white gentleman who walked up to my displays and said, "Thanks for being a part of history." Then turning, he briskly walked away. That gentleman's statement answered the question: *"What is Remembered?"*

Make Reenacting A Family Affair

EPILOGUE

Reenacting in Civil War reenactments has in store for those who embrace the hobby, a most deserving reward: the *good* feeling of being a "living historian" teaching American history "the way it was."

Another of the personal joys received from the hobby of reenacting is the opportunity to meet friendly people who represent both sides in the Civil War conflict. To hear stories from others about their family's ancestral roles, whether loyal to the Confederacy or to the Union, broadens understanding and *acceptance* of America's history.

At an Expo for the Florida Civil War Battle of Olustee, I presented a display featuring the role of "people of color" in the Civil War. Sharing the same tent with me was a lady engaged in spinning yarn with a spinning wheel; a cooper with his authentic colonial-made tools demonstrating his skills as a maker of barrels; and a tall, robust gentleman, authentically clad in Confederate gray with a fine display of Civil War weaponry. His display included a number of pistols, guns, mini balls, cannon balls, and other physical reminders of Civil War battles. My nerves cringed at the sight of long guns attached to long sharp bayonets. The mere sight of them, even while peacefully lying on a table, immediately transmitted a terrifying resemblance of shivers racing through me.

To quickly escape my frightful visions of Civil War battles where those sharp bayonets sliced through people, I turned away and questioned the comfort of the reenactor's wool gray uniform and asked how he acquired it. He described in detail the various parts of his uniform, citing how the heavy gray woolen clothing was not as uncomfortable as an observer might think, even in Florida's ninety-five degree heat. His garments, as required by the reenactment community, like all others, whether reenacting as a civilian, a Union or Confederate soldier, must have been made as authentically as possible, using fabric and styles of those worn during the Civil war years. While speaking with the gentleman about various and sundry things he said, "When God calls you home, you can not say, *I can't go.*"

"How true," I responded, "I like that."

Now, the reenactment community is calling people, "people of color" as well as all others, to come home to the hobby of reenacting. And many people *can* say, "I *can* go, I will like that."

The End

Notes About the Bibliography

The following is a list of recommended titles with notes to give reenactors, students, teachers and others a broader understanding of African-American history.

Historians through the years purposely left out documents in American history texts which proved that slaves and "free people of color" were not inherently inferior, but were human beings with intelligence and competent as skilled artisans in many trades. Although they were not considered as citizens, "people of color" made important contributions to the settlement and economic development of these United States. As reenactors, a knowledge of the past is essential to a fuller understanding of the role of "people of color" during the Civil War.

Facts about African-American history have been published, but cannot all be found in any one place. My conclusion: in order to learn the complete history of African-Americans, one must diligently search to find books to read and either borrow or purchase them. This list is an excellent reference source. Most titles can be ordered. Other than at public and school libraries, archives, college and university libraries, museums and historic sites are additional places to find books. Frequently, books about African-Americans rarely seen in book stores, can be found and purchased at museums and historic sites.

There is no avoidance of the requirement: reenactors, to be knowledgeable, *must* read to learn about the hobby and read to learn African-American history "the way it was."

(For the convenience of readers and especially librarians who may wish to consider ordering titles, a larger size font is used for ease in reading the annotations in the Bibliography.)

Selected Bibliography

Books in the following list, arranged in broad subject areas, are highly recommended for further reading. Background reading will enable reenactors to respond appropriately to comments from living history visitors who will question the participation of slaves and "free people of color" in the Civil war and question the cause of the war with regard to the issue of slavery.

The titles marked (+) will give reenactors knowledge to answer questions. Sections typed in bold print and marked (*) are of special interest for reenactors. Notes indicate titles appropriate for younger readers. Notes are omitted for a few publications which have titles that describe the books' contents. Out-of-print titles may be available through interlibrary loans.

General Reference
Reference Books for general coverage of African American History.

Bennett, Lerone, Jr. <u>Before the Mayflower, A History of Black America, The Classic Account of the Struggles and Triumphs of Black Americans.</u>+ NY: Penguin Bks., 1982.
  Bennett describes the Black family in the slave community, slave artisans, clothing, children, daily routine and countless other aspects of African American history from slavery through the Civil Rights Movement.

<u>Black Women in Nineteenth-Century American Life.</u>+ Edited by Burt James Loewenberg and Ruth Bogin. University Park, PA: Pennsylvania State University Pr., 1990.

Franklin, John Hope. <u>From Slavery to Freedom, A History of Negro Americans.</u>+ NY: McGraw-Hill, Inc., 1947.
  This comprehensive volume on the history of African Americans has been reprinted and revised in several new editions. It is an authoritative reference source which brings together facts in the history of the American Negro from his African beginnings to the present time. Its contents cover many topics to satisfy the needs of any one desirous of learning Negro history from a single volume.

Franklin, John Hope and Loren Schweninger. <u>Runaway Slaves, Rebels On The Plantation.</u> NY: Oxford University Press, 1999.
  Chapter titles: "The Plantation Household," "Backward Into Bondage," and "Profile of a Runaway." The authors describe in detail which slaves were likely to run away and the punishment fugitives received. Included are runaway advertisements and lists of persons who aided them. Included also are descriptions of the strategies used to catch and return runaways to the plantations.

Bibliography

Genovese, Eugene D. <u>Roll Jordan Roll, The World the Slaves Made</u>.+ NY: Vintage Bks., 1976.
    Chapter titles: "Life in the Big House," "Men of Skill," "Free Negroes" and "Clothes Make the Man and Woman." As the title suggests, the author describes in great detail the plantation life of slaves.

Glatthaar, Joseph T. <u>Forged in Battle, The Civil War Alliance of Black Soldiers and White Officers.</u> NY: Meridian Printing, 1991.
    The author covers: recruitment, training and discipline of the soldiers; also their coping with racism and prejudice in the service. The final chapter discusses "Life After the USCT." The appendix lists the Congressional Medal of Honor winners and black officers in the Union Army.

Gutman, Herbert. <u>The Black Family in Slavery and Freedom, 1750-1925.</u>+ NY: Vintage Bks., 1976.
    Gutman documents in great detail within charts and graphs facts about black family life from 1750-1925. A discussion of slave naming practices are included. This book will provide many hours of absorbed reading.

Jones, Maxine D. and Kevin M. McCarthy. <u>African Americans in Florida.</u>+ Sarasota, FL: Pineapple Press, 1993.
    This book includes chapters on slavery in Florida.

Jordan, Ervin L. Jr. <u>Black Confederates and Afro-Yankees in Civil War Virginia</u>. Charlottesville, VA: University of Virginia, 1995.
    This book is written from a point of view that may spark controversy. To obtain a balanced view of black participation in the Civil War, the published research of other authors in this bibliography should be consulted, specifically books by Berlin and Quarles.
    Jordan describes in detail the laws governing living conditions of free people of color and slaves in Virginia and how slaves and a few free Negroes served as fighters, body servants and in other non-combat roles in Confederate units during the Civil War. Virginia and Maryland had the largest population of free Negroes. A photograph of escaped Virginia slaves (contrabands) is included in the book.

Katz, William Loren. <u>Breaking the Chains, African-American Slave Resistance</u>. NY: Athenium Books, 1990.
    Katz quotes excerpts of slave narratives and weaves together informative chapters about slaves. Chapter titles: "A Troublesome Property," "Industrial and Urban Resistance," "Fiery Abolitionists," and "The Slaves' Civil War." The text is well-written to hold the attention of readers.

King, Wilma. <u>Toward the Promised Land, 1851-1861, From Uncle Tom's Cabin to the Onset of the Civil War.</u>+ (Milestones in Black American History Series.) NY: Chelsea Publishers, 1995.

Bibliography

Meir, August and Elliott Rudwick. From Plantation to Ghetto.+ NY: Hill and Wang, 1970.
> The authors discuss the effects of the historical experiences of generations of African Americans on their belief systems: their attitudes towards themselves and their ancestral homeland of Africa. African American readers of this text will be forced to examine their feelings in light of the social class in which they were compelled to occupy due to the perception of them as "inferior" by the ruling class.
> (See the Chapter, "Who me, I don't want to do that.")

Tobin, Jacqueline and Raymond Dobard. Hidden in Plain View, A Secret Story of Quilts and the Underground Railroad.+ NY: Anchor Bks., 2000.

Books for Young Readers

These titles are excellent for students of all ages. They help fill the void in African American history in school social studies textbooks.

Collier, Christopher and James Lincoln Collier. Slavery and the Coming of the Civil War, 1831-1861. The Drama of America History Series. NY: Marshall Cavendish, 2000.
> The authors explain in large print, the story of the slave trade, the slave South, The Missouri Compromise and the role of Abraham Lincoln in the slavery issue.

Cooper, Michael L. Slave Spirituals and the Jubilee Singers.* NY: Clarion Bks., 1950.

Day, Nancy. Your Travel Guide to Civil War America.*+ Minneapolis: Runestone Press, 2001.

Edwards, Pamela Duncan. Barefoot, Escape on the Underground Railroad.* NY: Harper Collins, 1997. (An easy book.)

Hansen, Joyce. Between 2 Fires, Black Soldiers in the Civil War. NY: Franklin Watts, 1993.
> Readers will find this book most interestingly written. It relates more than the number of black men who fought and died, but also includes a full explanation of the *conditions* under which they served in the Civil War. "Here is a richly detailed absorbing picture of the often unnamed, uncelebrated black soldiers who braved both enemy fire and the fire of prejudice to fight to preserve democratic ideas and --they hoped--to gain freedom and political rights for themselves and their children." (Quoted from the back cover.)

Howell, Donna W. Descriptions of Plantation Life.* Washington, DC: American Legacy Bks., 1997 Order from: American Legacy Bks., P.O. Box 1393B, Washington, DC 20013-1393.

Bibliography

Howell, Donna W. <u>The Lives of Slave Children.</u>* Washington, DC: American Legacy Bks., 1997. Order from: American Legacy Bks., P.O. Box 1393B, Washington, DC 20013-1393 (Includes photographs of slave children's clothing.) Suggested for school libraries.

Howell, Donna W. <u>Slave Auctions.</u>*+ Washington, DC: American Legacy Bks., 1997. Order from: American Legacy Bks., PO Box 1393B, Washington, DC 20013-1393. Suggested for school libraries.

Lester, Julius and Rod Brown. <u>From Slave Ship to Freedom Road.</u>* NY: Puffin Bks., 1998. (An easy book.)

Myers, Walter Dean. <u>Now Is Your Time, The African American Struggle for Freedom.</u>*+ NY.: Harper, 1991.
    Myers included in his book the true story of Al Rahman Ibrahima, the son of an African chief, who was stolen from Africa, shackled in chains, taken aboard a slave ship bound for America and sold as a slave to a planter in Mississippi. Ibrahima had been educated in Mali, a leading educational and cultural center. His story is documented in Congressional records. Among the slaves were educated people brought from the West coast of Africa.

Nofi, Albert A. <u>Untold History of the Civil War, The Underground Railroad and the Civil War.</u> Philadelphia: Chelsea House Publishers, 2000.
    This useful Civil War Chronology lists the main events of the Civil War. It precedes five attractively illustrated chapters: "Slavery in America," " The Rise of the Underground Railroad," "Some Notable Escapes," and "The Underground Railroad in the Civil War."

Polacco, Patricia. <u>Pink and Say.</u>* NY: Philomel Bks., 1994. (A Civil War Story.)

Stein, Conrad R. <u>The Story of the Underground Railroad.</u>* Chicago: Children's Press, 1981.* (An easy book.)

Thomas, Velma. <u>Freedom's Children, The Journey from Emancipation into the Twentieth Century.</u> NY: Crown Publishers, Inc., 2000.
    This is an Interactive Book featuring historical photographs and removable documents.

Winter, Jeanette. <u>Follow the Drinking Gourd.</u>* NY.: Knopf, 1988. (An easy book.)

Young, Robert. <u>The Emancipation Proclamation, Why Lincoln Really Freed the Slaves, Both Sides.</u> NY: Dillon Press. *+ 1994.

Note: Each of the above titles are highly recommended for school library collections.

Documents

These titles include <u>recorded</u> documentary evidence and eyewitness accounts of African Americans in America's history.

Bibliography

Fishel, Leslie H. and Benjamin Quarles. <u>The Negro American, A Documentary History.</u>+ Glenview, ILL: Scott, Foresman and Co., 1967.
    This vast collection of documents demonstrate that Negroes played a significant role in America's history. Included are numerous copies of documents that relate the primary role of the Negro in America's history.
    Chapter titles include: biographical sketches of Phyllis Wheatley, Benjamin Banneker, James Forten and others. Chapter titles related to topics covered in this guide are: "Role of the Negro in the Confederacy," "The House Slave and the Field Slave," Work patterns: "The Task System and the Gang System," "The Free Negro in the South." and "The Free Negro in the North."

Katz, William Loren. <u>Eyewitness, A Living Documentary of the African American Contribution to American History.</u>+ Rev. and Updated. NY: Simon & Schuster, 1995.
    This book quotes original documents relating to African Americans.

<u>We Are Your Sisters, Black Women in the Nineteenth Century.</u>+ Edited by Dorothy Sterling. NY: W. W. Norton, 1984.
    Chapter titles include: "Letters from Slave Women," "Part III The War Years," "Slavery Chain Done Broke at Last," and "Courtship and Family Life."

Genealogy

Extensive family history research provides an excellent course for discovering documents about slavery in one's own family. Titles of books for those with genealogy interest:

Fears, Mary L. Jackson. **<u>Slave Ancestral Research, It's Something Else.</u>**+ Bowie, MD: Heritage Books, 1995. **$30.00** Available from the author at 722 Mercedes Avenue, Daytona Beach, FL 32114

Gutman, Herbert. <u>The Black Family in Slavery and Freedom, 1750-1925.</u>+ NY: Vintage Bks., 1976.
    Title includes documented descriptions in great detail with charts and graphs depicting facts about Black family life in the years 1750-1925. The author's discussion of slave naming practices is of special interest to genealogists.

Thackery, David T. <u>Finding Your African American Ancestors.</u>+ Orem, Utah: Ancestry Publishing, 2000.
    Thackery includes resources for military records, published rosters and indexes for African American Regiments in the Civil War.

Biography

These books document incidents in the lives of persons who lived as slaves.

Bradford, Sarah. Harriet Tubman, the Moses of Her People.*+ Secaucus, NJ: Carol Publishing Group, 1997.
 This book includes Tubman's life experiences and role in the Civil War.

Douglass, Frederick. My Bondage and My Freedom.+ NY: Dover Publications, 1969.

Douglass, Frederick. Life and Times of Frederick Douglass, His Early Life as a Slave, His Escape from Bondage and His Complete History.+ NY: Macmillan Publishing Co., Inc., 1962

Jacob, Harriet. Incidents in the Life of a Slave Girl.*+ Cambridge: Harvard Univ. Press, 1987.

Keckley, Elizabeth. Behind the Scenes, or Thirty Years a Slave and Four Years in the White House.+ NY: Oxford Univ. Pr. 1988.
 Keckley includes her life experiences and service in the Civil War.

Krass, Peter. Sojourner Truth, Antislavery Activist.*+ NY: Chelsea House, 1988.
 Krass presents the life experiences of Sojourner Truth and her role in the Civil War.

McCurdy, Michael. Escape from Slavery, The Boyhood of Frederick Douglas in His Own Words.* N.Y. Knopf, 1994.
 This is a biography excerpted from Douglass' autobiography.

Slave Narratives
Slave Experiences told in the words of former Slaves.

Before Freedom, When I Just Can Remember, Twenty-seven Oral Histories of Former South Carolina Slaves. *+ Edited by Belinda Hurmence. Winston-Salem, NC: John F. Blair Publishers, 1989.

Bullwhip Days, The Slaves Remember, An Oral History. + Edited by James Mellon. NY: Avon Bks., 1988.
 Includes photographs of slaves and nurses who were house servants along with the slave narratives. One chapter highlights slave plantation experiences during the Civil War.

Lay My Burden Down, A Folk History of Slavery. Edited by B. A. Botkin. NY: Dell Publishing, 1973.

My Folks Don't Want Me To Talk About Slavery.*+ Edited by Belinda Hurmence. Winston-Salem, NC: John F. Blair Publisher, 1998.
 This is a text of slave narratives told by former slaves appropriate for elementary grade students.

Slave Narratives

Narrative of Sojourner Truth. +Edited and with an Introduction by Margaret Washington. NY: Vintage Bks., 1993.

On Jordan's Stormy Banks.+ Edited by Andrew Waters. Winston-Salem, NC: John F. Blair Publisher, 2000.

Slavery Time When I Was Chillun. *+ Edited by Belinda Hurmence. NY: G. P. Putnam's Sons, 1997.
Hermence quotes slave narratives with many photographs of slave children.

Slave Laws or Black Codes

Fishel, Leslie H. and Benjamin Quarles. The Negro American, A Documentary History.+ Glenview, ILL: Scott, Foresman and Co., 1967.

Bibliography
Slavery

Ball, Edward. Slaves in the Family.+ Farrar, Straus and Giroux, 1998.
Ball records in great detail his family's involvement in slavery. The reader learns from his book how the entire system operated: the family's ship trading business, their routes to Africa. the description of the tribes and how one tribe was selected in preference to others, how plantation records were kept, the author's meeting with the descendants of the slaves his ancestors owned, and much, much more. Slavery, how the system worked in several generations of the Ball family is the author's focus. A most interestingly written book.

Berlin, Ira, Editor. Remembering Slavery, African Americans Talk About Their Personal Experiences of Slavery and Emancipation.+ Published in conjunction with the Library of Congress. 1998. Book with 2 cassette tapes of slaves' voices.
Speaking of a most unusual book, this is it. Its companions are two cassette tapes with the voices of former slaves recorded. The reader/listener experiences the thoughts and feelings of those who were in bondage. In the 1930's, a Federal Writers Project engaged the work of writers (including Zora Neal Hurston) to interview former slaves. A few persons recorded their voices. These published interviews are called "slave narratives."

Cottman, Michael H. The Wreck of the Henrietta Marie, An African American's Spiritual Journey to Uncover a Sunken Slave Ship's Past.+ NY: Harmony Books, 1999.
A slave ship sank off the coast of Florida. The author and his deep sea diving comrades traveled the route of this ship, even from where the maritime records were stored in London, to the places where the ship was built, the guns built, the saloon where the crew came from, and followed the route of the ship from England to Africa to its final resting place on the bottom of the Atlantic Ocean. This book takes the reader vicariously on a fascinating journey aboard a slave ship.

Bibliography
Slavery

Jones, Jacqueline Jones. <u>Labor of Love, Labor of Sorrow, Black Women, Work and the Family from Slavery to the Present.</u> + NY: Basic Bks. Inc., 1985.
    Chapter titles: "My Mother Was Much of a Woman," "Slavery and Freed Women" and "The Civil War and Reconstruction."

Rivers, Larry Eugene. <u>Slavery in Florida, Territorial Days to Emancipation.</u>+ Gainesville, FL: University Press of FLorida, 2000.
    Rivers gives a comprehensive discourse on slavery in Florida.

Smith, Warren Thomas. <u>John Wesley and Slavery.</u>+ Nashville: Abingdon Press, 1986.
    Smith presents a brief summary of slavery in Chapter 1 in which he discusses: "The Conditions," "Life in the West Indies," "Slavery in North America." In addition, Smith in other chapters introduces: "John Wesley and His Family,"also "John Wesley Meets Black People." For a concise introduction to the topic of slavery, this 160-page book meets that description.

APPENDIX A
Reenactment Units

1st Kentucky Cavalry and Horse Artillery
http://www.users.kih.net/~dparker/

1st Michigan Colored Infantry (102nd USCT)
http://www.geocities.com/Athens/9425/102hp.html

1st South Carolina Volunteer Infantry (Colored)
http://www.awod.com/gallery/probono/cwchas/1sc.html

3rd United Stated Colored Troops   http://www.3rdusct.com/

4th U. S. Colored Infantry Regiment
http://www.ncwa.org/4thUS.html   (anl)

5th Regiment of the US Colored Cavalry
http://www.erols.com/browns

8th U.S. Colored Heavy Artillery
http://www.pages.about.com/mmadden4/index.html

12th U.S. Colored Heavy Artillery
http://www.bjmjr.com/civwar/12uscha.htm

14th Regiment, New York State Militia, Company E
http://www.nwdc.com/am14nysm

22nd U.S. Colored Heavy Artillery
http://www.22mass.com/

33rd New York Volunteers
http://www.magpage.com/~33dny/

54th Massachusetts Volunteer Infantry, Company I
http://www.awod.com/gallery/probono/cwchas/54ma.html

54th Massachusetts Volunteer Infantry - Company B
http://www.54thmass.org/

105th U.S. Colored Troops
http://www.awod,com/gallery/probono/cwchas/usct105.html

APPENDIX A
Reenactment Units

Links to various topics of interest to reenactors are listed at this web site: **http://www.coax.net/people/lwf/data.htm**

A few of the many topics are listed below:

CIVIL WAR READING LISTS
U.S. COLORED TROOPS
CAVALRY REGIMENTS
HEAVY ARTILLERY REGIMENTS

ORGANIZATION OF U.S. COLORED TROOPS BY STATES,
    BORDER STATES, NORTHERN STATES
HISTORY OF THE U.S. COLORED TROOPS
HISTORY OF AFRICAN AMERICANS IN THE CIVIL WAR
CIVIL WAR BATTLES

DEALING WITH SLAVERY
SLAVERY IN THE CIVIL WAR ERA
FREEDMEN, THE FREED SLAVE OF THE CIVIL WAR
DID BLACKS TYPICALLY SERVE AS CONFEDERATE SOLDIERS?

THE UNDERGROUND RAILROAD AND THE CIVIL WAR
THE SOUTH'S NEGRO REQUIREMENT
CIVIL WAR RELATED SITES IN THE NATIONAL PARK SERVICE
PICTURES OF THE CIVIL WAR

RECRUITS - REFUGEES   CONTRABANDS
BATTLES - SKIRMISHES - EXPEDITIONS
CIVIL WAR BATTLES - U.S. COLORED TROOPS
SUTLERS
UNION NAVY
BLACK SOLDIERS

APPENDIX B
Lincoln's Letter to Joshua F. Speed, August 25, 1855

"You suggest that in political action now, you and I would differ. I suppose we would; not quite as much however, as you may think. You know I dislike slavery and you fully admit the abstract wrong of it. So far there is no cause of difference. But you say that sooner than yield your legal right to the slave--especially at the bidding of those who are not themselves interested, you would see the Union dissolved. I am not aware that any one is bidding you to yield that right; very certainly I am not. I leave that matter entirely to yourself. I also acknowledge your rights and my obligations, under the Constitution, in regard to your slaves. I confess I hate to see the poor creatures hunted down, and caught, and carried back to their stripes and unrewarded toils; but I bite my lip and keep quiet. In 1841 you and I had together a tedious low-water trip, on a steamboat from Louisville to St. Louis. You may remember, as I well do, that from Louisville to the mouth of the Ohio there were on board, ten or a dozen slaves, shackled together with irons. That sight was continual torment to me; and I see something like it every time I touch the Ohio, or any other slave-border. It is hardly fair for you to assume, that I have no interest in a thing which has and continually exercises, the power of making me miserable. You ought rather to appreciate how much the great body of the Northern people do crucify their feelings, in order to maintain their loyalty to the Constitution and the Union."

"No man ever got closer to Lincoln than Joshua F. Speed. When Lincoln first went to Springfield in 1837, he shared a room with Speed over the latter's store."
Fragment, Aug. 1, 1858?
"As I would not be a slave, so I would not be a master. This expresses my idea of democracy. Whatever differs from this, to the extent of the difference, is no democracy." Lincoln

From Chapter III, "Lincoln And The Negroes," in <u>Lincoln His Words and His World</u> by the Editors of Country Beautiful, Waukesha, Wisconsin. MCMLXV. pp.32, 36

APPENDIX C

What a Price to Pay for Freedom

"My husband Julius Leach was a member of Co. D. 5th U.S. Colored Cavalry and was killed at the Salt Works VA. about six months ago...When my husband was killed my master whipped me severely saying my husband had gone into the army to fight against white folks and he, my master, would let me know that I was foolish to let my husband go he would "take it out on my back," he would "Kill me by piecemeal" and he hoped "that the last one of the nigger soldiers would be Killed" He whipped me twice after that using similiar expressions. The last whipping he gave me he took me into the Kitchen and tied my hands tore all my clothes off until I was entirely naked, bent me down, placed my head between his Knees, then whipped me most unmercifully until my back was lacerated all over; the blood oozing out in several places so that I could not wear my underclothes without their becoming saturated with blood. The marks are still visible on my back; On this and other occasions my master whipped me for no other cause than my husband having enlisted. When he had whipped me he said "never mind God dam you when I am done with you tomorrow you never will live no more. "I knew he would carry out his threats so that night about l0 o'clock I took my baby and travelled to Arnold's Depot where I took the Cars to Lexington I have five children. I left them all with my master except the youngest and I want to get them but I dare not go near my master knowing he would whip me again."[1]

Affidavit of Patsy Leach, 25 March 1865. *The Black Military Experience*

Belair (MD) Aug. 25th, 1864C[1]

The Slow Pace of Emancipation

Before 1776, Black slaves obtained legal freedom in America only as a gift from white owners or by buying themselves. Slavery was outlawed or curtailed in this order:

- 1777 Vermont
- 1780 Pennsylvania
- 1784 Rhode Island and Connecticut
- 1787 Northwest Territory (future Ohio, Indiana, Illinois, Michigan, Wisconsin, and part of Minnesota
- 1799 New York
- 1804 New Jersey

All steps taken by the above states provided for gradual emancipation only. Slavery lingered on in most of the Northern states through the 1840 Census, and in one, New Jersey--until 1860.

- 1820 Maine admitted as a free state and Missouri as a slave state in 1821
- 1846 Iowa admitted as a free state, balanced by Florida as a slave state in 1845
- 1850 California, admitted as free state, balanced by passage of the Fugitive Slave Law in 1850
- 1861 Kansas admitted as free state on the eve of the Civil War
- **1862** District of Columbia and in all the remaining western territories, ... slavery was abolished by Congress (Lincoln was the President)
- 1863 Emancipation Proclamation (Technical freedom given to all slaves in states in rebellion against the Union.)
- 1865 Thirteenth Amendment abolished slavery "within the United States or any place subject to their jurisdiction."

---

1. Thompson, Kathleen and Hilary Mac Austin, Editors. <u>The Face of Our Past. Images of Black Women from Colonial America to the Present.</u> Bloomington & Indianapolis: Indiana University Pr., 1999. p.97

2. "Negro History: The Bitter Years of Slavery," Reprint. Life Magazine, November 22, 1968. p.22.

APPENDIX D

Impressment of Free Negroes and Slaves

Senate Bill, No. 109.
An Act to Amend an Act Entitled
"An Act to Increase the Efficiency of the Army
by Employing Free Negroes and Slaves in Certain Capacities,"
Approved February 17th, 1864:

Page 1

 SENATE, November 22, 1864.—Read first and second times and ordered to be placed upon the calendar and printed.
[By Mr. HENRY, from Committee on Military Affairs.]

AN ACT
To amend An Act entitled "An Act to increase the efficiency of the army by employing free negroes and slaves in certain capacities," approved February 17th, 1864.

 1 SECTION 1. *The Congress of the Confederate States of America*
2 *do enact*, That the first section of said act be so amended as
3 to increase the compensation given to the free negroes and
4 other free persons of color named in said section to eighteen
5 dollars per month.

 1 SEC. 2. That the second section of said act be so amended
2 as to authorize the Secretary of War to empoly, for all the
3 purposes named in the first section of said act, forty thousand
4 slaves, instead of twenty thousand, as therein provided.

 1 SEC. 3. That the third section of said act be so amended
2 as to authorize the Secretary of War to impress forty thousand
3 slaves in case he shall be unable to procure their services
4 or hire as therein provided.

 1 SEC. 4. That the fourth section of said act be amended by

Page 2

2 adding thereto, that after free negroes are impressed, in
3 making impressments of slaves, those not engaged in agriculture,
4 manufacturing, and mechanical pursuits, shall be first
5 impressed, and in case there shall then be any deficiency,
6 further impressments of slaves shall be made by taking them
7 from those persons who have fifteen or more able-bodied field
8 hands between sixteen and fifty years of age.

APPENDIX D

Letter from J. H. Stringfellow

GLEN ALLEN, HENRICO, February 8, 1865

[President Davis:]

MY DEAR SIR: Impelled by the perils of our country and the thousand conflicting theories as to the cause and cure to continually have these things before me, I have been amazed to see that no one thus far have conceived, or if conceived had the boldness to present, in my judgement, the only solution of all these perils and difficulties. I address you because you have taken a long stride in the right direction, and because I believe your mind has already reached the true solution, but owing to peculiar circumstances has hesitated to enunciate it. The history of this war demonstrates the wonderful fact that the Confederate States mainly subsists both of the immense armies engaged in the conflict, and actually, after furnishing all the soldiers to one army, contributes about one-half of those making the army of its enemies, and should the war continue for another year the South will probably furnish two-thirds of the army of her foes. These facts which cannot be controverted, show certainly anything but weakness or inferiority on the part of the South; but it does not show that a change of policy in relation to the conduct of the war, and that a radical one; must be adopted or we shall be destroyed. Let us look at a few facts: The Yankees must now have in their service 200,000 of our ex-slaves, and under their next draft will probably have half as many more. We have not one soldier from that source in our ranks. It is held by us that slaves will not make soldiers, therefore we refuse to put them in the service, and I think are correct in so doing; but while we thus think and thus act our enemies are creating. In addition to their white force (which we have found to our cost in the last year to be quite as large as we could manage), an auxiliary army of own escape slaves of 300,000 or 400,000 men. Now, however, we may decry the negro as a soldier, every one knows that if the white troops of the Yankees are numerous enough to hold all ours in check, then this negro army can at will ravage and destroy our whole country and we will be absolutely conquered by our own slaves. We allege that slaves will not fight in our armies. Escaped slaves fight and fight bravely for our enemies; therefore a freed slave will fight. If at the beginning of this war all our negroes had been free does any one believe the Yankees would have been able to recruit an army amongst them? Does any know of a solitary free negro escaping to them and joining their Army? If our slaves were now to be freed would the Yankees be able to raise another recruit amongst them? If freedom and amnesty were declared in favor of those already in the Yankee lines would they not almost to a man desert to their old homes? Would not our freed negroes make us as good soldiers as they make for our enemies? Again, suppose we free a portion of our slaves and put them in the Army, we leave all the rest as a recruiting field for the enemy, from which we cannot get a single soldier, and thus we see one-half of our entire population of no avail to us, but on the contrary ready at every opportunity to join the ranks of our enemies.

Now, sir, Southern soldiers are the best that ever drew a blade in the cause of liberty, but there are some things which they cannot do; they cannot fight our battles against overwhelming numbers, and raise the necessary supplies for the Army and the women and children at home; and yet, sir, this is what they will be called upon to do if this war is protracted for two years longer. I ask, sir, then, In view of these facts, if the prompt abolition of slavery will not prove a remedy sufficient to arrest this tide of disaster? The Yankee Army will be diminished by it, our own Army can be increased by it, and our labor retained by it. Without it, if the war continues, we shall in the end by subjugated, our negroes emancipated, our lands parceled out amongst them, and if any of it be left to us, only an equal portion with our own negroes, and ourselves given only equal (if any) social and political rights and privileges. If we emancipate, our independence is secured, the white man only will have any and all political rights, retain all his real and personal property, exclusive of his property in his slave; make the laws to control the freed negro, who having no land, must labor for the landowner, and being an adequate supply of labor must work for the landowner on terms about as economical as though owned by him. We cannot

APPENDIX D
Letter from J. H. Stringfellow

consent to reconstruction even if they repeal all their laws and withdraw all their proclamations in regard to us, our lands, and our negroes, because they now have, or at any session of their Congress can make, the necessary number of States to alter the constitution in a constitutional manner, and thus abolish slavery and interfere in any other way they think proper. But even if the present Administration should pledge anything we may ask, it binds no one but themselves during their own term of service, which you of course understand better than I do; and suppose they should even promise, and stand by their promise, to pay us for our negroes, lost or to be emancipated, how will they pay us? They cannot by direct taxation, but only in levying an export duty on our products-cotton, tobacco, and naval stores; and this war has shown them and the world, if not us, how much they will bear, cotton commanding $1 per pound, tobacco $3, tar $200 per barrel, $c. To pay their war debt and free our negroes would make a debt of $6,000,000,000 or probably $8,000,000,000, the interest of which at 5 percent would take $4,000,000,000 of revenue to pay, and to raise something additional to extinguish the principal would require an additional $1,000,000,000. Thus, you can see an expert duty to this extent would be levied and could easily be raised upon our products; 20 cents upon cotton, which would make the price about 32 or 33 cents the world would pay, because they must have it and have bought it for much more, would bring an annual income of about $4,000,000,000 without counting the duty on tobacco and naval stores; but even with this most favorable view of the case, we should lose the whole of our own war debt, which is or will, be say, $2,000,000,000. Of course this would be repudiated, and justly, by our enemies if we consent to reconstruction; whereas if we emancipate we save the $2,000,000,000 and we can pay for the negroes $4,000,000,000 more and the export duty on cotton alone (which we should have levied if we go back into the Union) will pay the interest upon this at 5 per cent, and leave $1,000,000,000 as a sinking fund to extinguish the principal in some thirty or forty-years, and the slave-owner have all his labor on his farm that he had before (for, having no home and no property to buy one with, he must live with and work for his old owner for such wages as said owner may choose to give, to be regulated by law hereafter as may suit the change of relation).

And this $6,000,000,000 is not a debt we tax ourselves to pay, but the world pays it. The speculator who buys the cotton and pays the duty makes the manufacturer pay him his 10 or 15 percent net profit on his gross outlay; the manufacturer makes the merchant pay him his 10 or 15 percent on his gross outlay; the merchant charges the retail dealer his 10 or 15 per cent on his gross outlay and so on till the shirt is made, and he who wears it out pays the duty and all the different percentages upon it. Thus we will pay to the extent of our consumption of the exported article when manufactured and returned to us a mere nothing when compared to the immense gratuity, $6,000,000,000, which the world makes to us, and which they so justly should be made to hand over to us for the cold-blooded heartless indifference with which they have contemplated the bloody, inhuman, barbarous, and apparently hopeless contest in which we have been engaged, and which they at any moment could have arrested by a word. By emancipation I think we would not only render our triumph secure, as I have attempted to prove, in and of itself, but in all future time the negro, in place of being useless in time of war as a soldier, and really dangerous, as we have seen to our cost, continues to be an element of strength; and I think we may reasonably hope that the nations of the earth would no longer be unwilling to recognize us, for surely no people ever before struggled so long and under so many difficulties and endure so many privations so uncomplainingly as we have without finding some friendly hand outstretched to encourage or to help; and there can be no other reason than that we are exclusively and peculiarly a nation of slave holders. I think that even amongst our enemies numbers would be added to those who are already willing to go in peace, for we should thus give the lie at once and forever to the charge that we are waging a war only for negro slavery, and the heart of every honest lover of human liberty throughout the world would sympathize with the men who for their cherished rights of freemen would wage such an unequal contest as we have waged and besides sacrificing all their earnest convictions as to the humanity and righteousness of slavery, were willing to sacrifice their property interest of $4,000,000,000 to secure their independence, which might all be saved, so far as the promises of our enemies are concerned by reconstruction. In my judgement the only question for us to decide is whether we shall gain our independence by freeing the negro, we retaining all the power to regulate them by law when so freed, or permit our enemies through our own slaves to compel us to submit to emancipation with equal or superior political rights for our

APPENDIX D

Letter from J. H. Stringfellow

negroes, and partial or complete confiscation of our property for the use and benefit of the negro. And, sir, if the war continues as it is now waged, and we are forced, by the overwhelming odds of the Yankees and our own slaves in arms against us, into submission, it would be but an act of simple justice for the Yankee Government to see to it that their negro allies are at least as well provided for in the way of homes as those who have been arrayed in arms against them. I have always believed, and still believe, that slavery is an institution sanctioned, if not established, by the Almighty, and the most humans and beneficial relation that can exist between labor and capital; still I think that this contest has proven that in a military sense it is an element of weakness, and the teachings of Providence as exhibited in this war dictate conclusively and imperatively that to secure and perpetuate our independence we must emancipate the negro.

P. S. - We should the get rid of the only impediment in the way of an exchange of prisoners, thus getting, 30,000 or 40,000 more men in the field.
I have given you what I conceive to be the only solution to our difficulties. How to effect this is a serious difficulty. Men are reluctant-in fact it might be imprudent to discuss this thing publicly, but we know that in great crisis men think and act rapidly or at least should do so. If Congress would be convinced of the correctness of this course they could, in convention with the Governors of the States, devise some method by which conventions of the States could be held and the necessary measures adopted; first by law of Congress, if necessary, provide for paying the owners for them. I have not found a single slave-holder with who I have conversed but is willing to submit to the measure if deemed necessary by the proper authorities. Indeed, I have no doubts of the power of Congress as a military necessity to impress all of the able-bodied male negros and pay for them, giving them their freedom, and providing for paying for the rest upon the condition of manumission, but the other course would be less objectionable. We burn an individuals cotton, corn, or meat to keep it from the enemy, so we can take his negro man and set him free to keep him from recruiting the enemy's Army.

I have written you this much hoping it may aid you in some way. I have shown what I have written to no one, nor communicated my intentions to any one. If you think what I have written worth anything, make what use of it you choose. If not, just stick it between the bars of your grate. What I have written is with an honest endeavor to aid you in guiding our ship through the perils and darkness which surround her, and from no feeling of dissatisfaction or distrust as to yourself, for you have all my sympathies and all of my trust and confidence. With difficulties and the warmest admiration and respect, I remain your friend.

J. H. STRINGFELLOW

P. S. - Written very hurriedly and with no effort at arrangement but only as "food for thought."
J. H. S.

I opened the envelope to say that my communication was written before I heard of the return of our commissioners, and that I am more than sustained by their report and the action of the Yankee Congress on the slavery question, and now we have only to decide on or between emancipation for our independence or subjugation and emancipation, coupled with negro equality or superiority, as our enemies may elect.
J. H. S.
[Indorsement]
Respectfully referred, by direction of the President, to the Honorable Secretary of War.
BURTON N. HARRISON
Private Secretary
SOURCE: United States War Department. THE WAR OF THE REBELLION: A Compilation of the Official Records of the Union and Confederate Armies. Series IV, Volume III. Washington: Government Printing Office, 1880-1901.

APPENDIX E
Marlboro Jones, Body Servant

It is estimated that there were tens of thousands of African-Americans, like Marlboro Jones, who marched and camped with Confederate armies. They occasionally fought as cooks, body servants, and camp servants. "Some of these men, like Jones, wore uniforms; until the act of March 1865, only a few were formerly enlisted as cooks or servants and they were not "soldiers" in the usual understanding of the term."

Captain Randal F. Jones of the 7th Georgia Cavalry was the slave master of Marlboro Jones. As a faithful servant, Jones "brought his master home to Savannah after he was mortally wounded at Trevilian Station, Virginia in 1864...."

The Museum of the Confederacy, Richmond, Virginia

APPENDIX F
Female Slave Contrabands

For an understanding of the contrast between the acceptance of slave males in both armies and non-acceptance of female slaves, information is given for female reenactors who select the role of "female slave contrabands." The following quotes are excerpted from "Female Slave Contrabands in the Civil War" in <u>A Woman's War, Southern Women, Civil War and the Confederate Legacy.</u> Edited by Edward D.C. Campbell, Jr. and Kym S. Rice. Charlottesville: Museum of the Confederacy, Richmond, 1996. pp.59, 60, 61.

"Manning the home fires in the South and in the North, white women took on the tasks of managing and sometimes working farms and plantations raising children alone, nursing the wounded and keeping up morale amid death and growing hunger and despair." White women knitted socks, and made other necessities for Confederate soldiers as their patriotic duty.

...."With no hearths of their own to protect and without lawfully recognized spouses, fathers, or sons to nurse, cheer on in battle, worry about, or grieve for--female slaves in the eyes of whites did not merit even the unofficial, temporary standing accorded Northern and Southern white women in the war."

...."the wives, mothers, daughters and sisters of black soldiers found their efforts rebuked and Federal guarantees of protection rarely honored."

"On plantations and farms and in urban areas, they (slave women) hastened freedom's arrival by refusing any longer to defer to mistresses or masters..." On both sides of the conflict, black men were considered valuable for "building fortifications, digging ditches, cutting roads and canals through swamps, cooking and cleaning." Others were enlisted as Union soldiers. As soldiers, there was no parallel role for women. However, "the South first drafted female slaves to nurse, cook, and clean in Confederate hospitals."

"Neither side believed that slave women had any real part to play in the conflict." Some Union soldiers desired to return them to their masters. For protection, the female slave contrabands and their children lived in makeshift settlements near Union camps. These were sometimes raided and destroyed by Confederates.

Thousands of slave women and children became contrabands by merely living on plantations in southern areas where the Union army came as they pushed into Confederate territory. Thousands of others continued to flock into Union lines seeking freedom and protection. Although they did not find themselves in a safe haven or sanctuary, they found freedom.

NAME INDEX

A
Andrew, John A., 58, 113
Attucks, Crispus, 107
Auld, Hugh, 57

B
Babcock, James Mrs., 10
Barton, Clara, 51
Baumfree, Isabella, 53, See also Sojourner Truth
Bectom, John C., 2
Biddle, Nicholas, 106, 107
Birdsong, Yvette, 47, 91
Bliss, Brian, 120
Booker, Pepper, 154
Booker, Joyce, 69
Bowser, Mary Elizabeth, 41, 42
Bowser, Wilson, 42
Butler, Benjamin, 26
Brockington, Barbara, 120
Brown, William Wells, 55
Bridges, Robert, 43

C
Caldwell, Pinkie, 120
Cary, Mary Ann Shad, 56
Cotton, Anisha, 5

D
Dabbs, Loretta, 46, 125
Davis, Jeff, 3
Davis, Jefferson, 48, 99, 129
Delany, Martin Major, 58
Douglass, Charles, 58
Douglass, Frederick, 34, 50, 55, 57, 58, 108, 113
Douglass, Lewis, 58
Dovel, Dwight, 120

E
Edmondson, Emily, 40
Edmondson, Mary, 40
Ellison, April, 22
Ellison, William, 22
Ely, Andrew F., 97

F
Fears, Joel V. Jr., 32
Fears, Joel V. Sr., 32, 84
Fears, Mary, 70, 126
Finnegan, General, 53
Finnegan, Joseph General, 110
Forten, Charlotte, 34, 43, 44, 51, 52 71, 103, 113
Forten, James, 43, 71, 128
Frazier, Michael Rev., 59
Frazier, Michael, Jr., 81
Frazier, Zaporah, 81
Fribley, Charles Colonel, 109

G
Garland, Mr., 47, 48
Garrison, William Lloyd, 43, 49
Gooding, James Henry, Corporal, 97
Gordon, 92, 93, 94
Grant, Ulysses S. General, 42, 58

H
Hague, Eric, 97
Hammond, James H., 68
Heichold, A. P., 110
Herndon, Tempe, 17
Higginson, Thomas Wentworth, 44, 108
Holmes, Mat, 3

I - J
Jackson, 92, 93
Jackson, Edith, 74
Jacobs, Harriet, 49, 56
Jarrett, Douglas, 101
Jasper, John 78
Johnson, Andrew President, 59
Johnson, Ernestine, Frontispiece, 37, 96, 101

K
Keckley, Elizabeth, 34, 47, 48, 50, 70, 96, 103
King, Karl, 112
King, Edward Sergeant, 53
King, Ezekiel, 2, 3

NAME INDEX

L
Laino, Jesus, 92
Leach, Patsy, 144
Lewis, E., 97
Lincoln, Abraham, 3, 22, 44, 49, 50, 55, 57, 58, 59, 107, 108, 113, 143
Lincoln, Mary Todd, 49, 50
Lincoln, Willie, 49
Livermore, Mary, 12

M
McClean, Mrs., 49
McFadden, 2
McMillan, Alma, 4
McNeil, Mary, 2
Mitchell, Kenneth O., 61, 96
Montgomery, James Colonel, 38
Murphy, Lucy, 2

N
Nelson, Martha, 97
Nicholson, Merceda, 43
North, Oliver E. 97

O

P
Patterson, Jane, 65, 80
Patterson, Oscar, 4
Peake, Mary Kelsey, 46
Pierce, Clifford, 4, 113, 118, 119
Pierce, Jacquelyn, 4
Peden, John, 112, 118, 119
Purvis, Harriet, 43
Purvis, Robert, 43

Q - R
Reed, Dolly, 52
Reid, Mel, 113, 114, 115
Remond, Charles L., 55
Rone, Sarah, 36, 96
Ruffin, Josephine, 56

S
Sereg, Eugene, 120
Seymour, Truman General, 110
Shakespeare, 85
Shaw, Robert Colonel, 44, 113
Small, Lydia, 61
Smalls, Robert, 61, 62
Smith, Matherlyn, 56
Smith, Virginia, 41
Speed, Joshua, F. 143
Stanton, Edwin, 59
Stringfellow, J. H. 129, 146
Susanna, 51

T
Taylor, Susie King, 31, 34, 51, 52, 96 103, 128
Thames, Azza, 51
Truth, Sojourner, 31, 35, 55
See also Baumfree, Isabella
Tubman, Harriet, 34, 37, 38, 55, 96, 101, 102, 128
Turner, Henry McNeal, 59
Turner, Mel, 111

U - V
Van Lew, Elizabeth, 41, 42
Vaughn, Leon, 112

W
Walker, 48
Ward, Janome, 79
Whittier, John Greenleaf, 42
Woodhouse, Mrs., 52
Wooten, Robert, 2

X - Y - Z
Yates, Sharon R., 70
Young, Carah, 81

*Who Fills The Shopping Spaces
At Civil War Reenactments?
Sutlers*

Invest in the Best

Fig. 74. Reenactor Pepper R. Booker Visiting a Sutlery

Booker is holding a vest in front of a sutlery at a Civil War reenactment. One obligation of old timers and persons new to the hobby, is to invest in all that is necessary to become a successful interpreter. Investing in authentic wearing apparel for both civilian and military reenactors can best be accomplished by visiting sutleries. There are many.

For the civilians, they sell all clothing items and accessories from hats to shoes. For the military, they sell all uniforms, weaponry and accouterments. For a fine representation, sulteries are prepared to assist reenactors to invest in the best.

Not only are ready-made clothing available, but there are Civil War seamstresses with expertise, not only in making garments, but also, in knowledge about Civil War period fabric and where to get it. (See the ads that follow.)

ABOUT THE AUTHOR

MARY L. JACKSON FEARS, a graduate of Bethune-Cookman College and Florida State University with a Bachelor and Masters Degree respectively, is the author of *Slave Ancestral Research, It's Something Else*, a work credited by Dr. Charles L. Blockson of Temple University as "fact written in the prose style surpassing even the Haley fictional account with regard to historical veracity and authenticity." She is the author of two other books: *Julie's Journey* and *The Jackson-Moore Family History and Genealogy*.